TOAD
OF TOAD HALL

A Play from
Kenneth Grahame's Book
"The Wind in the Willows"

by

A. A. MILNE

The Music

by

H. FRASER-SIMSON

SAMUEL   FRENCH

LONDON
NEW YORK TORONTO SYDNEY HOLLYWOOD

© (No. 85402) 1929 by Charles Scribner's Sons
© 1932 (Acting Edtiion) by Samuel French Ltd
© 1960, in Renewal, by Dorothy Daphne Milne

1. *This play is fully protected under the Copyright Laws of the British Commonwealth of Nations, the United States of America and all countries of the Berne and Universal Copyright Conventions.*

2. *All rights, including Stage, Motion Picture, Radio, Television, Public Reading and Translation into Foreign Languages, are strictly reserved.*

3. **No part of this publication may lawfully be reproduced in ANY form or by any means—photocopying, typescript, recording (including video-recording), manuscript, electronic, mechanical, or otherwise—or be transmitted or stored in a retrieval system, without prior permission.**

4. Rights of Performance by Amateurs are controlled by Samuel French Ltd, 52 Fitzroy Street, London W1P 6JR, and they, or their authorized agents, issue licences to amateurs to give performances of this play on payment of a fee. **It is an infringement of the Copyright to give any performance or public reading of the play before the fee has been paid and the licence issued.**

5. Licences are issued subject to the understanding that it shall be made clear in all advertising matter that the audience will witness an amateur performance; that the names of the authors of the plays shall be included on all announcements and on all programmes; and that the integrity of the author's work will be preserved.

The Royalty Fee indicated below is subject to contract and subject to variation at the sole discretion of Samuel French Ltd.

> Basic fee for each and every
> performance by amateurs   Code M
> in the British Isles

In Theatres or Halls seating Six Hundred or more the fee will be subject to negotiation.

In Territories Overseas the fee quoted above may not apply. A fee will be quoted on application to our local authorized agent, or if there is no such agent, on application to Samuel French Ltd, London.

The publication of this play does not imply that it is necessarily available for performance by amateurs or professionals, either in the British Isles or Overseas. Amateurs and professionals considering a production are strongly advised in their own interests to apply to the appropriate agents for consent before starting rehearsals or booking a theatre or hall.

ISBN 0 573 05019 8

TOAD OF TOAD HALL

Originally produced by William Armstrong at the Playhouse, Liverpool, on the 21st December 1929, then at the Lyric Theatre, London, on the 17th December 1930, and subsequently at the Savoy Theatre, London, on the 22nd December 1931, with the following cast of characters—

(in the order of their appearance)

MARIGOLD	*Nova Pilbeam*
NURSE	*Mona Jenkins*
MOLE	*Richard Goolden*
WATER RAT	*A. Cameron Hall*
MR BADGER	*Eric Stanley*
TOAD	*Frederick Burtwell*
ALFRED	*R. Halliday Mason*
THE BACK LEGS OF ALFRED	*Frank Snell*
CHIEF FERRET	*Neal Aiston*
CHIEF WEASEL	*Robert Hughes*
CHIEF STOAT	*Leslie Stroud*
FIRST FIELD-MOUSE	*Jim Neal*
SECOND FIELD-MOUSE	*Jim Soloman*
POLICEMAN	*Alban Blakelock*
GAOLER	*Robert Hughes*
USHER	*Beeson King*
JUDGE	*Tom Reynolds*
TURKEY	*Jim Soloman*
DUCK	*Jim Neal*
PHOEBE	*Wendy Toye*
WASHERWOMAN	*Dorothy Fane*
THE WHITE RABBIT	*Wendy Toye*
MAMA RABBIT	*Phyllis Coulthard*
LUCY RABBIT	*Daphne Allen*
HAROLD RABBIT	*Jim Neal*
FOX	*Jim Soloman*
BARGE-WOMAN	*Muriel Johnston*

Ferrets, Weasels, Stoats, Rabbits, Squirrels and Field-mice

SYNOPSIS OF SCENES

PROLOGUE
Down by the Willows

ACT I
The River Bank

ACT II
SCENE 1 The Wild Wood
SCENE 2 Mr Badger's House
SCENE 3 The same (some weeks later)

ACT III
SCENE 1 The Court-House
SCENE 2 The Dungeon
SCENE 3 The Canal Bank

ACT IV
SCENE 1 Rat's House by the River
SCENE 2 The Underground Passage
SCENE 3 The Banqueting-room at Toad Hall

EPILOGUE
The Wind in the Willows

The vocal score is published and on sale.   Band parts can be obtained on hire from Samuel French Ltd.

TOAD OF TOAD HALL

PROLOGUE

No. 1

SCENE—*Down by the Willows. A warm morning in Spring. (See Photograph of Scene)*

> Wind in the willows is whispering low,
> Still is the meadow which dreams in the sun,
> Blue overhead and green your bed,
> Sleep, little people, to Lullaby.
>
> Down where the river winds heavy and slow
> Sleep, now the chase of the morning is done,
> Blue overhead and green your bed,
> Sleep, little people, to Lullaby.
>
> Wind in the willows is whispering low,
> Still is the meadow which dreams in the sun,
> Blue overhead and green your bed,
> Sleep, little people, to Lullaby.

(*As the* CURTAIN *rises,* NURSE *can be heard singing off* L. *After a short while she enters and seats herself beside a willow tree* LC. *She is knitting a sock, but before long seems to have fallen asleep over it. This leaves* MARIGOLD (*who is twelve*) *to amuse herself. She is sitting on a grass mat* RC *and talking down the telephone. At least she has the trumpet of one daffodil to her ear, and of another to her mouth, and has apparently just got on to the exchange*)

MARIGOLD. Hallo, is that the Exchange? I want River Bank one-double-nought-one . . . (*Lying on her front, facing* R) Hallo, is that the Water Rat's house? . . . Oh, I *beg* your pardon. They've given me the wrong number . . . Oh, Exchange, you've given me the wrong number. I wanted Mr Rat's house and you've given me Mr Badger's. (*To herself*) Sorry, you've been tr-r-roubled . . . Hallo, is that the Water Rat's house? Is that Mr Rat speaking? Good morning, Mr Rat, this is Marigold speaking . . . Yes, isn't it a delightful day? . . . Yes. Well, almost alone. Nurse is here, but she's asleep.

(NURSE *opens her eyes*)

How's Mr Mole? . . . Oh, haven't you seen him? I expect he's

1

very busy spring-cleaning. You see, when your house is *all* base-ment, there's such a lot of spring-cleaning to be done . . . Yes, I prefer a river-side residence too . . . May I really come one day? How lovely . . . No, not tomorrow, I'm having tea with Mr Toad . . . Yes, conceited, but *so* nice . . .

NURSE (*who was not asleep*) Well, really, Marigold, you do think of funny things.

MARIGOLD (*hurriedly*) Oh, Nurse is awake. Good-bye. (*She puts down the telephone, rises on her knees and faces Nurse—sternly*) Have you been overhearing, Nurse?

NURSE (*nodding*) And wondering at you, dearie. Who ever heard the like?

MARIGOLD. It's very bad manners to overhear a perfectly private telephone conversation.

NURSE. Couldn't help it, dearie, you're that funny—with your Mr Rat and Mr Toad and all, just as if they were yooman beings——

MARIGOLD. Well, but so they are.

NURSE (*surprised at this*) Yooman beings?

MARIGOLD. Yes. I mean they are as human to themselves as —as we are to us.

NURSE (*after a gallant effort*) No, it's no good, dearie, I can't follow it.

MARIGOLD (*crossing to R of Nurse, kneeling, and leaning on Nurse's knees*) I mean, they must *seem* quite big and grown up and human to each other.

NURSE. Now fancy that!

MARIGOLD. Mr Toad, he's all puffed out and conceited, but very nice, you know, and very sorry afterwards for talking so much about himself. (*She faces front*) And Mr Rat's a dear—that's him I was talking to just now. He's very quick and clever and helpful, and his little sharp eyes are always looking out so as to see that he doesn't hurt people's feelings. And Mr Mole—I'm not sure about *him*. You see, he lives underground a good deal, and doesn't go out into society much, so I should think he'd be rather simple, and not liking to talk about himself, and just saying "Yes" and "No", and waiting to be asked before he has a second cup. And then Mr Badger—of course he's grey, and much older than the others, and very fatherly—and sleeps a good deal with a hand-kerchief over his face, and when he's woken up, he says, "Now, now, now" and (*she yawns*) "Well, well, well."

NURSE. Well, well, well, fancy that now! Why, you might almost have seen them at it, the way you talk.

MARIGOLD. I have. (*She moves to front of Nurse, kneels, and leans back on Nurse's knees, looking up*)

NURSE. Never!

MARIGOLD. Yes. One morning. I came out here early, oh ever so early. Nobody was up—you weren't up, and the birds weren't up, and even the sun wasn't up—and everything was so still that there was no sound in all the world, except just the wind in the willows, whispering ever so gently.

NURSE (*professionally*) What your poor mother would have said—— (*Eagerly*) Well, and what happened?

MARIGOLD. I don't know. I sat there and waited for everything to wake up, and then by and by I heard something—music, very thin and clear and far off—and then—well, then there was the sun, and it was daylight, and it seemed as if I had just woken up myself. But it was all different.

No. 2

Something had happened. I didn't know what, but I seemed to understand more than I did before—to have been *with* them. (*She rises and speaks to front with sudden excitement*) Wouldn't it be lovely if they suddenly came out and began to talk (*she points* R)— Mole from under the ground there, (*she points* L) and the Water Rat from his hole in the bank, (*she points at back stage* C) and the old Badger from the dead leaves in the ditch, and Mr Toad—— (*She faces front*)

NURSE. I should be that frightened, if they were all big.

MARIGOLD (*turning back to Nurse and putting her arms round her*) Oh, no, you wouldn't, because they wouldn't know *we* were here. We should just listen to them, without their knowing anything about it. (*She turns and calls out*) Mr Mole! Mr Rat! Mr Toad! Oh, Nurse, wouldn't it be *lovely*?

NURSE. Oo, I can hear something! Listen!

MARIGOLD. That's the music again. Quick! Hide!

(MARIGOLD *crosses* R, *then comes back for* NURSE, *and they both exit* R.)

(*It is dark suddenly, and we hear music, very thin and clear and far off: "the horns of Elfland faintly blowing"*)

ACT I

SCENE—*The River Bank.* (*See Photograph of Scene*)

Gradually it grows light again. There is no NURSE, *no* MARIGOLD *now. But somewhere at the back there is a curious upheaval going on. The earth moves and humps up and falls back again. Somebody is at work underneath. We hear breathings and mutterings. In a little while we can distinguish words. It is old friend* MOLE.

MOLE (*from behind the bank up stage* C) Scrape and scratch and scrabble and scrooge—scrooge and scrabble and scrape and scratch—up we go, up we go! . . . Pop! (*He stands up and comes down the bank*) Ah! (*He takes a deep breath of daylight*) This is fine! (*He goes to* R, *then to* L) This is better than whitewash. Hang spring-cleaning! Oh, what a day! Oh my, oh my, oh my! Blow spring-cleaning! (*He rubs his eyes with his paw, and crosses to down stage* RC) Is that a River? Oh my, oh my! *Bother* spring-cleaning!

No. 3

(*From the front door up* LC, WATER RAT *appears. He has bright eyes and a sharp friendly face, with whiskers*)

RAT (*at end of dance, up stage,* LC) Hallo, Mole!

MOLE (R *of Rat*) Hallo, Water Rat!

RAT. Don't seem to have seen you about before. (*He comes down* LC *and lies down, facing front*)

MOLE (*shyly*) I—I don't go out much, as a rule.

RAT (*cheerily*) Prefer home-life? *I* know. Very good thing too in its way.

MOLE. Yes, you see, I—— (*He comes down* RC) This is a river, isn't it?

RAT. *The* River.

MOLE (*simply*) I've never seen a river before.

RAT (*staggered*) Never seen a—— You never—— Well, I—— What *have* you been doing then?

MOLE. Is it as nice as that?

RAT. Nice? My dear young friend, believe me, it's the *only* thing. There is *nothing*—absolutely nothing—half so much worth doing as simply messing about by a river. (*Dreamily*) Simply messing—messing about by a river—or *in* a river—or *on* a river. It doesn't matter which.

MOLE. But what do you *do?*

RAT. Nothing. Just mess about. That's the charm of it; you're always busy, and yet you never do anything in particular; and when you've done it, there's always something else to do, and

4

you can do it if you like, but you'd much better not . . . And so you've never even *seen* a river before? Well, well!

MOLE (*timidly*) I am afraid you must think me very ignorant.

RAT (*kindly*) Not at all. Naturally, not being used to it. (*He rises*) Look here, what are you doing today?

MOLE (*hesitatingly*) I—I *was* spring-cleaning.

RAT. On a day like this!

MOLE. That's just it. Sometimes I seem to hear a voice within me say "Whitewash," and then another voice says "Hang whitewash!" (*Slowly*) And I don't quite know which of the—I don't quite know—I don't qui—— Oh, *hang* whitewash! (*He turns* R *and throws away the brush which he has in his hand*)

RAT (*crossing* R *to Mole and patting him encouragingly*) That's the spirit. Well, what I was about to suggest was a trifle of lunch on the bank here, and then I'd take you round and introduce you to a few of my friends. Does that appeal to you at all?

MOLE (*ecstatically*) Does it appeal to me? Does it? Oh my, oh my, oh my! (*He turns round*)

RAT (*soothingly*) There, there! You don't want to get *too* excited. It's only just a trifle of lunch. Cold tongue—cold ham—cold chicken—salad—french rolls—cress sandwiches—hard-boiled eggs—bloater paste—tinned peaches—meringues—ginger beer—lemonade—milk chocolate—oranges—— Nothing special—only just——

MOLE (*crossing from* R *to* L, *then back to* LC) Stop, stop! Oh my! oh my! Oh, what a day!

RAT. That's all right. You'll feel better soon. Now just you wait here—don't go falling into the river or anything like that—and I'll be back in two minutes with the luncheon-basket.

MOLE (*wiping away the tears*) Oh Mr Rat, my generous friend,

(RAT *moves up to his front door and exits*)

I—I—words fail me for the moment—I—(*he holds out his hand*)—your kindness—that expression, if I caught it correctly, "luncheon-basket"—a comparative stranger like myself—did I hear you say "bloater paste"?—you—I—— (*He opens his eyes and finds that Rat has gone*) Oh! (*He moves over* R, *then comes back again and sits behind the tree-trunk* L) Oh, what a day!

No. 4

(*It is indeed a day. For suddenly the leaves begin to move beneath him, and* MOLE *rises and falls with the motion of a small boat on a choppy sea. A final upheaval dislodges him altogether, the leaves scatter and disclose the recumbent form of* MR BADGER. *Slowly he humps himself into a sitting position, then stands up.* MOLE *runs round, followed by* BADGER. *At the end of this* BADGER *is* LC *and* MOLE R *of him*)

BADGER (*gruffly*) Now the *very* next time this happens I shall be exceedingly angry. I have had to speak about it before, and I don't want to speak about it again. But I will *not* have people sitting down on me just as if I were part of the landscape. Now who is it this time? Speak up!

MOLE. Oh, please, Mr Badger, it's only me.

BADGER. Well, if it's only you, that makes a difference. I don't want to be hard on you. But I put it to you that when an animal is being particularly busy underneath a few leaves, thinking very deeply about things——

(RAT *emerges with the lunch*)

More company; oh, these crowds! (*He moves down* L)

RAT. Here, Mole, give us a hand with this basket.

(MOLE *moves up to* R *of* RAT, *and together they bring the basket to down* C)

Hallo! Why, it's Mr Badger!

BADGER. Ah, Ratty, my dear little man, delighted to see you. I was just telling this little fellow——

RAT (L *of the basket*) By the way, let me introduce you. My friend, Mr Mole.

BADGER (*down* L) Don't mention it. Any friend of yours, Ratty——

MOLE (*down* R, *timidly*) How do you do, Mr Badger? I am very proud to meet you. I'm sure I'm extremely sorry——

BADGER (*crossing* R *to Mole*) That's all right, that's all right. Any friend of Ratty's may sit down *where* he likes and *when* he likes, or I'll know the reason why. (*He crosses* L *again*) Well, and what are you two little fellows doing?

RAT (*moving to* R *of the basket*) Just having a trifle of lunch. Stay and join us, won't you?

MOLE (*crossing up and round to* L *of the basket—shyly*) Oh do, Mr Badger! It's a picnic! (*He helps* RAT *with the basket*)

BADGER. H'm! Picnics aren't much in my line. Got company coming?

RAT. Only Mole and myself. Unless Toad happens along.

MOLE (*in an ecstatic whisper, going to Badger*) There's cold tongue—cold chicken—salad—french rolls—cress sandwiches—hard-boiled eggs——

BADGER (*crossing to the basket*) Well, if you're sure there's no company. You know, Ratty, I never did like society. (*He sits down heavily on the basket, much to* MOLE's *disappointment, who was hoping to get to work at once*)

RAT (*crossing down* R *and sitting*) Can't say I see much in it myself.

BADGER. Sensible animal. And what about your friend Mr Mole?

MOLE (*sitting down* L) Oh, I live a *very* quiet life, Mr Badger. A field-mouse or two drops in from time to time—perhaps half a dozen of them will come carol-singing at Christmas—but beyond that I hardly see anybody.

BADGER. That's right. Ratty, your little friend promises well.

RAT (*rising and moving back to the basket*) Yes, but you're sitting on the lunch, and we can't——

(MOLE *also edges towards the basket*)

BADGER (*taking no notice*) He has the right ideas. (*Solemnly*) How different from *one* whom we could mention!

RAT. Oh, Toad? Toady's all right.

BADGER (*shaking his head sadly*) Ah me!

MOLE (*rising*) I have heard of the great Mr Toad. It would be a privilege to make his acquaintance.

RAT. Oh, you'll see him all right. He's sure to be along soon.

(RAT *and* MOLE *pull the straps on each side of the basket*)

BADGER. And when you see him, my little friend, take warning by him. Society has been his undoing.

(MOLE *pulls again*)

RAT. Well, I wouldn't say that. I—— (*He also gives another pull*)

BADGER. If it were not for the desire to shine before his acquaintances, what a much more dependable animal Toad would be! I knew his father.

(RAT *pulls*)

I knew his grandfather.

(MOLE *pulls*)

I knew his uncle, the Archdeacon——

(RAT *turns* R)

What his poor father would have said——

RAT (*cheerily*) Hallo, Toady! (*He moves* R *slightly, waving a paw*) I thought he'd come along soon.

No. 5

(TOAD *comes in boisterously from* L, *as full of himself as usual. He does a dance behind the tree-trunk* L)

TOAD (*at end of dance*) Hallo, you fellows! This is splendid! (*He jumps over the tree-trunk to Badger*) Hallo, old Badger! Dear old Ratty! (*He shakes Rat warmly by the paw*) Hallo! (*He seizes Mole's paw and works it up and down*) And dear old Badger! (*He passes back to Badger again*) How are you?

BADGER. So-so.

TOAD. Splendid, splendid!

RAT. My friend, Mr Mole.

TOAD (*going back enthusiastically to Mole*) How are you? (*He shakes his paw vigorously*) Splendid, eh? That's good. (*He goes to Rat*) And old Ratty. (*He goes to Badger*) *And* Badger.

BADGER. We were talking about you, my young friend.

TOAD (*spreading himself with delight*) Ah well, the penalty of fame. Eh, Ratty? One gets talked about. One is discussed. One is a topic of conversation. (*He swaggers down* L) One is speculated about. There it is. One can't help it. (*He crosses to Rat*) Well, Ratty, old man, and how are you?

RAT. *I'm* all right. We were just going to have a trifle of lunch. (*He goes round the basket to* L *of it,* R *of Mole*) You'd better join us. (*He pulls at the basket again*) I say, Badger, old man——

TOAD. No, no, you all come up to *my* house. Come up to Toad Hall. *I'll* give you lunch, the finest lunch you ever had.

MOLE (*crossing to Toad, unable to imagine anything superior to Rat's effort*) But there's cold tongue—cold ham—cold chicken—salad —french rolls—cress sandwiches—hard-boiled sandwiches——

TOAD. Pooh! Wait till you've seen mine. Ratty knows. Eh, Ratty? They're quite famous—been referred to in books. (*He swaggers across* L) "Another select little luncheon-party at Toad Hall." That sort of thing.

MOLE (*awed*) Oh! (*He looks anxiously at Rat, to whom, after all, he is engaged for lunch*)

RAT. Now, now, Toad!

BADGER. Well, I'll be moving. (*He rises slowly and crosses* R)

(MOLE *goes to* R *of the basket*)

RAT (*getting to the basket at last*) Thanks, old chap.

TOAD. That's right. We'll all be moving. (*To Mole*) It's only a step to Toad Hall. Jacobean residence—with bits of Tudor. Finest house on the river. You'll like it.

MOLE (*eagerly*) I'm sure I shall.

BADGER (*to Mole*) Good-bye, my young friend. We shall meet again. And before very long, if I'm not mistaken. Good-bye, Ratty.

RAT. Sure you won't stay to lunch?

TOAD. But you are coming to lunch with *me*, old Badger.

BADGER (*severely*) Nobody is coming to lunch with you, Toad. Many a time I have lunched at Toad Hall with your father; an animal of few words, but of what an intellect! Ah me! How different from—but I shall refer to that later. Good-bye, my unhappy young friend.

(BADGER *goes out heavily down* R)
(TOAD *goes to the bank up* C)

MOLE (*anxiously*) Isn't Mr Badger feeling very well?

TOAD (*recovering himself*) Poor old Badger, he gets that way sometimes. No fire, no spirit, no—what's the word—*élan*.

(RAT *goes up* LC)

Well, well, we can't all have it. Hallo, Ratty, where are you off to?

RAT (*disappearing through his front door*) The corkscrew.

TOAD (*not moving*) Now, let *me* fetch it. (*To Mole*) Tell you what (*coming down to behind the basket* c), you must come and stay with me. Let me put you up at Toad Hall.

MOLE. It's very kind of you, but——

TOAD. That's all right. Plenty of room at Toad Hall. Open house for my friends. Always glad to see them. (*He jumps over the basket and sits in front*) Now what have we got for lunch? (*He assumes the position of host*) Try one of these sandwiches. (*As* RAT *emerges with the corkscrew and comes to* L *of the basket*) Come along, Ratty, try one of these sandwiches. Got the corkscrew? Good. (*To Mole*) Let me open you one of these bottles. Sit down, Ratty; make yourself comfortable.

RAT (*quietly to Mole*). Got everything you want?

MOLE (*sitting* R *of the basket*) Yes, thank you.

RAT (*sitting* L *of the basket*) That's right. Well, Toady, and what have you been doing lately? Boating? Haven't seen you on the river this last day or two.

TOAD. The river! Boating! Bah! Silly boyish amusement, I've given that up *long* ago. Sheer waste of time. No, I've discovered the real thing, the only genuine occupation.

RAT. What's that? Help yourself, Mole.

TOAD. Aha, what is it? Come to Toad Hall and you shall see.

MOLE. Oh, do let's.

RAT. All right, we'll drop in one afternoon.

TOAD. Drop in? One afternoon? Nonsense! You're coming to stay. Always welcome, that's my motto. I've had it picked out in green on the front-door mat. "Always welcome. A home from home." (*To Mole*) You'd like to come, wouldn't you?

RAT. Sorry, but Mole is staying with *me*.

TOAD. Now, you dear good old Ratty, don't begin talking in that stiff and sniffy sort of way, because you know you've got to come.

(RAT *tries to speak*)

And don't argue; it's the one thing I can't stand. You surely don't mean to stick to your dull fusty old river all your life and just live in a hole in the bank? Come and stay with me, and I'll show you the world.

RAT (*rising and giving a ginger bottle to Toad*) I don't *want* to see the world. And I *am* going to stick to my old river, *and* live in a hole, just as I've always done. And I'm going to teach Mole all about the river, aren't I, Mole? And Mole is going to stick to me and do as I do, aren't you, Mole? (*He goes to down* L *and lies down*)

MOLE (*loyally*) Of course I am. I'll always stick to you, Rat.

(*Wistfully*) All the same, it sounds as though it might have been —well, rather fun at Toad Hall.

Toad. Fun? Wait till you see what I've got. I've got the finest—— Well, wait till you see it. Pass the sandwiches, Mole, there's a good fellow. (*To Rat*) Seen any of the Wild-Wooders lately?

Rat. No.

Mole. Who are the Wild-Wooders?

Rat (*pointing across the river*) They live over there in the Wild Wood.

(Mole *crosses to* l *of Rat and sits*)

We don't go there very much, we River-Bankers.

Mole. Aren't they—aren't they very nice people in there?

Toad. They daren't show their noses round Toad Hall, that they daren't. I'd soon send them packing.

Rat. The squirrels are all right. And the rabbits. Of course there are others. Weasels and stoats and ferrets, and so on. They're all right in a way—I'm very good friends with them——

Toad. So am I.

Rat. But they break out sometimes, there's no denying it. And if they don't like you, they—well, they show it.

Toad. I wouldn't ask them to Toad Hall, not if they sat up and begged me to. I'm not afraid of them; I just don't like them. Pass the meringues, Mole, there's a good fellow.

No. 6

(*But* Mole *has risen and gone* r, *staring beyond Toad at something strange which is approaching them from* l—*a gaily painted caravan drawn by an old grey horse*)

Rat. What is it, Mole?

Mole. Whatever's that?

(*They turn*)

Alfred (*the horse—up stage* lc, *after dance*) Oh, there you are. I've been looking for you everywhere.

Toad (*down* c, *excitedly*) Now isn't this lucky? Just at the psycho —psycho—what's the word?

Alfred (*hopefully*) Encyclopaedia. That is, if you ask *me*.

Toad. I didn't ask you. Ratty, *you* know the word——

(Rat *rises*)

Alfred. Introduce me to your friends, won't you? I do get so frightfully left out of it.

Toad. My friends Mr Mole and Mr Rat. This is Alfred.

Alfred. Pleased to meet you. If you're coming my way, you must let me take you. Only I do like a little conversation. (*To*

Toad) Encyclopaedia, that was the word you wanted. (*He comes down and sits on the tree-trunk*)

RAT (*sadly*) So this is the latest?

TOAD (*eagerly*) Absolutely the very latest. There isn't a more beautiful one (*crossing to Mole*), a more compact one, a more—what's the word?——

ALFRED. Heavy.

TOAD. A more up-to-date one, a more——

RAT (*crossing* R *to Toad*) So this is the latest craze! I understand. Boating is played out. He's tired of it, and done with it.

ALFRED. Don't blame *me*. I wasn't consulted about this at all; but if I had been, I should have said Boats. Stick to Boats.

TOAD. My dear old Ratty, you don't understand. Boating—well—a pleasant amusement for the young. I say nothing against it. But there's real life for you—(*he waves a paw at the caravan*) in that little cart. The open road, the dusty highway, the heath, the common, the hedgerows, the rolling downs!

ALFRED. *And* the ups.

TOAD (*crossing* L, *then up stage to the caravan*) And mind, this is the very finest cart of the sort that was ever built, without any exception. (*He opens the caravan*) Come inside and look at the arrangements, Mole. Planned 'em all myself, I did.

MOLE (*timidly to Rat*) We could just look inside, couldn't we? It wouldn't—wouldn't *mean* anything.

ALFRED (*airily*) Nothing! Nothing!

RAT (*reluctantly*) Oh well, we may as well look at it, now we *are* here.

(RAT *and* MOLE *move up to the caravan*)

TOAD. All complete! You see—biscuits, potted lobster, sardines—everything you can possibly want. Soda-water here—baccy there——

(TOAD *shows them into the caravan*)

(*Emerging again*) Bacon, jam, cards, dominoes—you'll find that nothing whatever has been forgotten.

ALFRED (*with feeling*) I've noticed it.

TOAD. Well, what do you think of it, Mole?

(*All three are now up stage,* RAT RC, MOLE C *and* TOAD LC)

MOLE. It's lovely!

TOAD. Glad you like it. What about starting this afternoon? Come on, Mole, give us a hand—— (*He moves down to above the basket* C)

(ALFRED *rises and crosses above the basket to down* R)

MOLE (*torn between the two of them*) Oh, Ratty!

TOAD. Come on, Ratty, old fellow. This is the real life for a gentleman.

(MOLE *comes down to help pack the basket*)

Talk about your old river! (*He begins packing up the lunch*)

RAT (*down* RC) I *don't* talk about my river. You *know* I don't, Toad . . . But I *think* about it. I think about it—all the time.

MOLE (*crossing to Rat and squeezing his paw*) I'll do whatever you like, Ratty. We won't go. I want to stay with *you*. And—and learn about your river.

RAT. No, no, we'd better see it out now. It wouldn't be safe for him to go off by himself. It won't take long—his crazes never do.

ALFRED (*coming between Rat and Mole*) When *I* was young, it was considered bad manners to whisper, and leave people out of conversations.

(MOLE *crosses to* L *of the basket*, RAT *to* R *of it*)

(*In a loud conversational voice*) My own view—since asked—of the climatic conditions, is that the present anti-cyclonic disturbance in the——

TOAD. Ah! Shall I help? . . . That's right . . .

(RAT *and* MOLE *take the lunch-basket up to the caravan and put it inside*)

All aboard? Here, we're forgetting the corkscrew. Will you get it?

(MOLE *trots back for it*)

Don't bother. *I'll*—— Oh, you've got it. Good.

(RAT *moves down to Alfred, and backs him up stage into the shafts*)

Now then, are we all ready? You get up there, Mole.

(MOLE *sits on the shafts on one side of the caravan*)

You on the other side, Ratty? Or would you rather——

(RAT *remains at the horse's head*)

Oh, are *you* going to lead him? I will, if you like. Sure you don't mind? Right, then I'll get up here. Now then, right away!

(*They start off*)

ALFRED (*to Rat*) You mark my words. No good will come of this. But don't blame *me*. That's all. Don't blame *me* afterwards. Psychological—that was the word he wanted. Not encyclopaedia. I thought it seemed funny somehow. Psychological.

No. 6a

(*The caravan goes out* R)

∗   ∗   ∗   ∗   ∗

No. 7

(*It grows dark. A thunderstorm, you would say, is brewing. In the darkness scuffling noises can be heard: breathings. It becomes lighter, and now we can see. The* Wild-Wooders *are here!* Ferrets, Weasels, Stoats *perform weird evolutions as they chant their terrible war-song*)

> Toad! Toad! Down with Toad!
> Down with the popular, successful Toad!

(*The three* Chief Conspirators *form a mystic circle in the middle and utter this horrid incantation*)

Chief Ferret. O may his bathroom cistern spring a leak!
Chief Weasel. On Sunday morning may his collar squeak!
Chief Stoat. May all his laces tie themselves in knots,
Chief Ferret. And may his fountain pen make frequent blots!
Chief Weasel. May he forget to wind his watch at night—
Chief Stoat. And may his dancing-pumps be *much* too tight!

(*They dance solemnly*)

The Ferrets. Every ill which Toad inherits
        Will be welcomed by the Ferrets—
All. Down with Toad! Down with Toad!
The Weasels. Day and night the elder Weasels
        Hope that he will have the measles—
All. Down with Toad! Down with Toad!
The Stoats. How the happy little Stoats
        Laugh when he is off his oats!
All. Down with Toad! Down with Toad!
        Toad! Toad! Down with Toad!
        Down with the popular successful Toad!

(*It grows darker again. The* Wild-Wooders *can still be heard chanting their diabolical refrain, but they can no longer be seen. There is a loud clap of thunder; it is daylight again; the* Wild-Wooders *have vanished. Then the "poop-poop" of a motor-car is heard, followed by a loud crash. Suddenly* Alfred *enters from up stage* R *at a gallop, followed by* Mole)

Mole (*soothingly to Alfred*) There, there! . . . There, there!

(*But* Alfred *refuses to "there, there!" He careers round the stage with the broken ends of the shaft attached to him, pursued by the conciliatory* Mole)

There, there! It's all right, Alfred. (*Very reassuringly*) It's all right.

(Rat *comes in, supporting a dazed* Toad. *They cross to* LC)

Rat (*turning and shaking his fist at something*) You villains! You scoundrels, you highwaymen, you—you——

Alfred (*still gyrating* l *of Rat and Toad*) Road-hogs. That's the word. Always come to me if you want the right word. Road-hogs.

Rat. You road-hogs. I'll have the law of you! Rushing about the country at fifty miles an hour! I'll write to all the papers about you! I'll take you through all the Courts! (*He turns anxiously to Toad*) How are you feeling now, Toady? Mole, come and give us a hand with poor old Toad. I'm afraid he's pretty bad.

Mole (*down* r, *catching up Alfred at last*) There, there! That's all right now, isn't it? (*He goes to Rat*) Poor old Toad! (*He takes his other arm, and together he and* Rat *conduct the dazed one to the tree-trunk* l)

(Toad *sits on the tree-trunk*)

Alfred. I said that no good would come of it, and now you see. A cataclysm—that's what the whole thing's been.

Rat (l *of Toad—anxiously*) Speak to us, Toady, old man! How is it?

Toad (*staring in front of him with a rapt expression*) Poop-poop! . . . Poop-poop! . . . Poop-poop!

Mole (r *of Toad*) What's he saying?

Rat. I *think* he thinks he's the motor-car.

Toad. Poop-poop!

Mole (*soothingly*) It's all right, Mr Toad. It's all right now.

Rat. We'll make 'em sit up, Toad. We'll have the law of 'em. We'll get you another little cart—we'll make 'em pay for it.

Toad. Poop-poop! . . . (*He rises and moves to* c) Glorious, stirring sight! The poetry of motion! The *real* way to travel! The *only* way to travel! Here today—in the middle of next week to-morrow! Oh bliss, oh rapture! Oh poop-poop!

Rat. Oh, stop being an ass, Toad!

Toad (*dreamily*) And to think that I never knew!

Rat (*going to* lc) Now, look here, Toad, pull yourself together. We'll go to the police-station, and lodge a complaint, and we'll go to a wheelwright's and have the cart mended.

Toad. Police-station? Complaint! *Me* complain of that beautiful, that heavenly vision which has been vouchsafed me? *Mend* the *cart*? I've done with carts for ever. Horrid little carts, common carts, canary-coloured carts!

Mole (*hopelessly*) What are we to do with him?

Rat (*sadly*) I see what it is. I recognize the symptoms. He is in the grip of a new craze.

No. 7a

(*Faintly the* Ferrets *and the* Stoats *and the* Weasels *are heard singing* "Down with Toad! Down with Toad! Down with the popular, successful Toad!")

Toad (*raptly*) Poop-poop!

(Toad *turns round and goes off* L, *above the tree-trunk, but re-enters again down* L *almost immediately. He crosses* R *and goes off*)

Rat (*to Mole*) Well, come along. Let's get him home.

(Rat *follows Toad off*)

Mole. Come on, Alfred.

(Alfred *goes up stage and round to down* L. *He then crosses* R *and goes off, followed by* Mole)

(*As soon as they are gone, the Bank is alive again with the* Wild-Wooders, *who burst into mocking laughter*)

Curtain

ACT II

Scene 1

No. 8

Scene—*The middle of the Wild Wood.* (*See Photograph of Scene*)
*It is an awesome place in the moonlight, with the snow thick upon the
ground: cold, silent, threatening. Yet not altogether silent, that is the
worst of it. You feel that there are hidden watchers behind the trees,
waiting to jump out at you; you hear, or seem to hear, their stealthy
movements. There is a sudden rustling . . . and then silence. A twig
cracks. Somebody is breathing . . .*

Now at last we can recognize somebody. It is Toad, *in motoring gloves
and goggles, coming anxiously through the trees from* l, *with many a
sudden stop and furtive glance over his shoulder. We can hear, and he
hears too, a murmur of unseen voices, which rises in a sort of chant until
at last we can distinguish the words.*

Chorus of Wild-Wooders. Toad! Toad! Down with Toad!
Down with the popular, successful Toad!
Toad (*alarmed*) W-what's that?

(*Mocking laughter answers him*)

Pah!

(*Dead silence*)

I said "Pah!" (*Nervously*) A-and "Bah!" (*Loudly*) Bah!

(*There is an echoing* "Bah")

What's that?

(*Again the echo of the last word comes back to him, and he laughs, but
a little uneasily*)

Silly of me. Just an echo. Something to do with the acoustics.
Listen. (*He puts his hand to his mouth*) Rat!

(*Dead silence*)

Perhaps it doesn't work sometimes. Something to do with the
direction of the wind. I'll try again. (*Very loudly*) Rat!
A Solemn Voice. Mole!

(*And then a burst of laughter off* l. Toad *hides behind the ground
row* rc)

Chorus (*in quick, business-like time*) Toad! Toad! Down with
Toad!
Down with the terrified and timorous Toad!

TOAD (*coming back to* C) C-c-come and do it! C-come and do it if you dare.

(*The mocking laughter again off* L)

Yes, that's all you can do—laugh. Anyone can laugh. Ha-ha-ha-ha! Very funny, isn't it? (*He moves* R)

A VOICE (*off* R) Where are you going, Toad?

TOAD (*coming back to* C) Never you mind where I'm going. (*More confidently as he thinks of Badger*) I'm going to see Badger, that's where I'm going.

(*There is another burst of laughter*)

A VOICE (*off* R) Badger doesn't live here, Toad.

TOAD (*desperately, greeting an imaginary friend*) Yes, he does, there he is. Ah, my dear Badger, how *are* you? No, not at all. Yes, delighted, quite so, no, yes, not in the least. Fancy! Ha, ha! Well, yes, just a little walk through the wood. Oh, do you think so? And you're looking splendid yourself. Never saw you look fiercer. (*Loudly*) I said *fiercer!* (*As he goes off*) This way, my dear Badger!

(*There is a last shout of laughter as* TOAD *disappears off* L)

No. 8a

CHORUS (*softly*) Toad! Toad! Down with Toad!
Chilblains and Mumps to the Miserable Toad!
Toad! Toad! Down with Toad!
Frostbite and Hiccups to the Miserable Toad!

(*The chant goes on, a murmur of unseen voices, whose words we can no longer distinguish. In a little while we can hear nothing, and yet it seems that at any moment we shall hear something. No wonder that* MOLE, *limping through the trees from* L, *keeps looking over his shoulder*)

MOLE (LC, *hopefully*) Ratty! (*In sudden panic as a bat crosses the stage from* R *to* L) What's that? Pooh! It's nothing! *I'm* not frightened! . . . I do wish Ratty was here. He's so comforting, is Ratty. Or the brave Mr Toad. He'd frighten them all away. (*He seems to hear the sound of mocking laughter off* L) What's that? (*He looks round anxiously*) Ratty always said, "Don't go into the Wild Wood." That's what he always said. "Not by yourself," he said. "It isn't safe," he said. "We *never* do," he said. That's what Ratty said. But I thought I knew better. There he was, dear old Rat, dozing in front of the fire, and I thought if I just slipped out, just to see what the Wild Wood was like—what's that——? (*He breaks off suddenly and turns up stage, fearing an attack from behind. There is nothing*) I should be safer up against a tree. Why didn't I think of that before? (*He settles himself at the foot of a tree up* LC) Ratty would have thought of it, he's so wise. Oh, Ratty, I wish you were here! It's so much more friendly with two! (*His head droops on his chest*)

A Voice (*from far off* R) Moly! Moly!

Mole (*waking up suddenly*) What's that?

A Voice (*nearer*) Moly!

Mole (*frightened*) Who is it?

A Voice. Moly! Moly! Moly! Where are you? It's me—it's old Rat!

(Rat *enters* R, *and crosses to Mole* LC. *He has a lantern in his hand and a cudgel over his shoulder.* Mole *is crawling around distraught*)

Mole (*almost in tears*) Oh, Rat! Oh, Rat!

Rat (*patting him on the back*) Moly! Moly! There, there, there!

Mole. Oh, Ratty, I've been so frightened, you can't think.

Rat. *I* know, *I* know. You shouldn't have gone and done it, Mole. I did my best to keep you from it. We River-Bankers hardly ever come, except in couples.

Mole. But *you've* come by *your*self. Ah, but then that's because you're so brave.

Rat. It isn't just bravery, it's knowing. There are a hundred things you have to know, which we understand about, and you don't as yet. Of course if you're Badger, it's different.

Mole. Surely the brave Mr Toad wouldn't mind coming here by himself?

Rat (*laughing*) Old Toad? He wouldn't show his face here alone, not for a whole hatful of guineas, Toad wouldn't.

Mole. Oh, Rat! It is comforting to hear somebody laugh again.

Rat. Poor old Mole! What a rotten time you've had. Never mind, we'll soon be home now.

Mole (*sitting*) Oh, Ratty. I don't know how to tell you, but I'm afraid you'll never want me for a companion again, but I can't, I simply *can't* go all that way now.

Rat. Tired?

Mole. Aching all over. Oh, Ratty, do forgive me. I feel as if I must just sit here for ever and ever and ever, and I'm not a bit frightened now you're with me—and—and I think I want to go to sleep.

Rat. That's all right. But we can't stop *here*. (*He looks round about him*) Suppose we go and dig in that mound there, and see if we can't make some sort of a shelter out of the snow and the wind, and have a good rest. And then start for home a bit later on. How's that?

Mole (*meekly*) Just as you like.

Rat. Come on, then. (*He crosses* R, *in front of the ground row and makes preparations to dig*)

(Mole *follows, but barks his shins and sits down with a squeal*)

Mole. Oh, my leg! Oh, my poor shin! Oo!

Rat. Poor old Mole, you don't seem to be having much luck today, do you? What is it? Hurt your shin? (*He brings the lantern*) Let's have a look at it.

Mole. I must have tripped over a stump or something. Oh my! Oh my!

Rat. It's a very clean cut. That was never done by a stump. Looks like the sharp edge of something metal. Funny!

Mole. Well, never mind what done it. It hurts just the same whatever done it.

Rat. Wait a moment. (*He begins scratching in the snow in front of the ground row*)

Mole. What is it?

Rat. I thought so!

Mole (*still nursing his leg*) What *is* it?

Rat. Come and see.

Mole (*hobbling up*) Hullo, a door-scraper! How very careless of somebody!

Rat. But don't you see what it means?

Mole (*sitting down again and rubbing his shin*) Of course I see what it means. It means that some *very* forgetful person has left his door-scraper lying about in the middle of the Wild Wood just where it's sure to trip everybody up. Somebody ought to write to him about it.

Rat. Oh, Mole, how stupid you are! (*He begins scratching busily again*) There! What's that?

Mole (*kneeling, with his back to the audience, and examining it closely*) It looks like a door-mat.

Rat. It *is* a door-mat. And what does *that* tell you?

Mole. Nothing, Rat, nothing. (*He turns to front*) Whoever heard of a door-mat telling anyone anything? They simply don't do it. They are not that sort at all. They—what have you found now?

(Rat, *still at it, has now disclosed a solid-looking little door, dark green, with a brass plate on it*)

Rat (*rising, proudly*) There! (*He fetches the lantern and holds it up to the plate*) What do you read there?

Mole (*also rising, awestruck*) "Mr Badger. Seventh Wednesdays" . . . Rat!

Rat (*proudly*) What do you think of *that*?

Mole (L *of the ground row, facing* R) Rat, you're a wonder, that's what you are! I see it all now. You argued it out step by step from the moment when I fell and cut my shin, and you looked at the cut, and your majestic mind said to itself, "Door-scraper." Did it stop there? No. Your powerful brain went on working. It said to itself——

Rat (*impatiently*) Yes, yes, well now, let's——

No. 9

MOLE (*going on sleepily and happily*) Your powerful brain said to itself, "Where there's a scraper, there must be a mat."

RAT. Quite so. And now——

MOLE (*facing front*) "I have noticed before," said the wise Mr Rat,

"That where there's a scraper there must be a mat."

(*To Rat*) And did you stop *there*? No. Your intellect still went on working. It said grandly to itself, "Where there's a door-mat there must be a door."

RAT. Exactly. And now that we've found it——

MOLE (*lying down, facing front*) Said the wise Mr Rat, "I have noticed before,

That where there's a door-mat there must be a door."

You know, Rat, you're simply wasted here amongst us fellows. If I only had your head——

RAT. But as you haven't, I suppose you are going to sit on the snow and *talk* all night. Now wake up a bit and hang on to this bell-pull, while I hammer.

MOLE (*sleepily, rising*) Oh, all right!

Said the wise Mr Rat, "I have often heard tell

That where there's a bell-pull there *must* be a bell."

(MOLE *hangs on to the bell-pull, while* RAT *hammers on the door with his cudgel. Down in Mr Badger's house a deep-toned bell responds*)

CURTAIN

SCENE 2

No. 9a

SCENE—*Badger's Underground Home.*

The room which we see is one of those delightful mixtures of hall, kitchen, drawing-room, dining-room, larder and pantry. In the middle of the room stands a long table of plain boards on trestles, with benches drawn up to it. There is a big open fireplace with high-backed chairs on each side. The floor is brick; from the rafters hang hams, nets of onions and bundles of herbs. In short, a place where heroes can feast after victory, harvesters keep their Harvest Home with mirth and song, and two or three friends sit about as they please in comfort and content. There are three doors, labelled FRONT DOOR, BACK DOOR, *and* STUDY. (*See Photograph of Scene*)

(*At the rise of the* CURTAIN, BADGER *is discovered in the armchair* R *of the fireplace, asleep, "The Times" over his face, and his feet up on the armchair opposite. At a knocking on the Back Door a convulsion passes over "The Times"; at a second knocking it stands on end; and at a third* Mr Badger *comes out from behind the leading article. Grumbling to himself, for his after-supper nap has been disturbed, he goes to the door* L)

Badger (*opening the door*) Well, well, well, what is it, what is it?

(*A collection of* Field-mice, *half a dozen of them in red mufflers, stand nervously shuffling at the entrance*)

First Field-mouse (*down* L) Oh, please, Mr Badger, did you want any carols?

Badger (LC) Any *what*? Speak up!

First Field-mouse (*swallowing*) Carols.

Badger. Let's have a look at them.

Second Field-mouse (*striking up*) "Good King Wenceslas looked out——"

(*He is* R *of* First Field-mouse, *other* Field-mice *being grouped behind*)

Badger. Oh, I thought you said carrots. Run along, all of you. Time you were in bed.

Second Field-mouse. "Good King Wenceslas looked out——"

Badger. And if you come round disturbing *me* again, *you'll* have to look out. Now then, off you go.

First Field-mouse. Oh, please, Mr Badger, we always used to sing carols to Mr Mole, and he used to ask us in, and give us hot drinks, and supper too sometimes.

Second Field-mouse (*proudly*) We had steak-and-kidney pudding once.

First Field-mouse. That's right, sir.

Second Field-mouse. Real steak-and-kidney pudding with kidney in it.

First Field-mouse. That was Mr Mole, sir. Down at Mole End. Always asked us in, Mr Mole did.

Badger. Ah! Mole did, did he? And Mole is a very sensible young animal. I have great hopes of Mole. Well, run away now, but come back in twenty minutes, when I'm not so busy, and perhaps I'll let you sing me the—what did you call it?

Field-mice (*eagerly*) Carol.

Badger. Carol. I thought you said carrot. Well, then, you can sing me the one that Mr Mole liked, and if I like it too, I won't say that perhaps there won't be a bit of hot something for one or two of you, the ones that don't snuffle, that is, and——

Field-mice. Oh, thank you, Mr Badger.

Badger. Now then, run along, there's good children.

(*The* Field-mice *shuffle out through the door* L)

So Mole likes carols, does he? (*He goes back to his chair, and picks up the paper*) Likes carols, does he? Carols . . . Thought he said carrots.

(*The front-door bell rings. There is a hammering, too, at the door. Very much annoyed,* BADGER *gets to his feet and goes* R *to the door*)

All right, *all* right, *all* right! What is it, who is it? (*He opens the front door*) Speak up!

RAT. Hallo, Badger! It's me, Rat, and my friend Mole, and we've lost our way in the snow, and Mole's that tired you never did.

BADGER. Well, well, well! Rat and his friend Mole!

(BADGER *brings them in.* RAT *goes to* RC, MOLE *to down* R)

Come along in, both of you, at once. Why, you must be perished! Well I never! Lost in the snow! And your friend that tired! Well, well! And in the Wild Wood at this time of night! I'm afraid you've been up to some of your pranks again, Ratty. (*He goes to the door* R *and closes it*) But come along in. There's a good fire here, and supper and everything.

(MOLE *crosses in front of Badger to the chair above the table* RC. RAT *goes to the fireplace*)

MOLE (*as he sees the supper-table*) Oo, I say!

BADGER (*crossing to the armchair* R *of the fireplace*) Now what will you do first? Toast your toes a bit? (*He removes "The Times"*) I was just glancing at the paper. Or supper now, and toast your toes afterwards? It's all ready. I was expecting one or two friends might drop in.

MOLE (*shyly*) I think I should like supper at once, please, Mr Badger. (*He sits in the chair above the table*)

BADGER. That's right, Mole. Sensible animal. (*He sits in the armchair* R *of the fireplace*) And what about you, Rat?

RAT (*who is standing with his back to the fire, as an old friend should*) Just as you like. (*He crosses to the table for a sandwich*) Fine old place this, isn't it, Mole?

MOLE (*already among the plates*) Grand.

BADGER (*to Rat*) Won't your friend try some of those pickles?

RAT (*crossing back to the fireplace*) Try a pickle, Mole.

MOLE (*his mouth full*) Thanks. (*He helps himself*)

BADGER (*solemnly, after a silence broken only by the noise of eating*) I've been wanting to see you fellows, because I have heard very grave reports of our mutual friend, Toad.

RAT (*sadly*) Oh, Toad! (*He shakes his head*)

MOLE (*as sympathetically as he can with a mouth full of pickles*) Tut-tut-tut.

BADGER. Is his case as hopeless as one has heard?

RAT. Going from bad to worse—that's all you can say about him, isn't it, Mole?

MOLE (*nodding busily*) 'M! (*He swallows hastily*) That's all.

RAT. Another smash-up only last week, and a bad one. You see, since he's got this motor craze, he's convinced he's the greatest driver ever, and nobody can teach him anything. And so it goes on.

MOLE. And so it goes on.

BADGER (*gloomily*) And so it goes on! (*After a pause*) How many has he had?

RAT. Cars or smashes? Oh well, it's the same thing with Toad. The last was the seventh. (*He sits in the armchair* L *of the fireplace*)

MOLE (*still busy*) You really ought to try a slice of this beef, Rat.

RAT. No, thanks, really.

MOLE. Don't know when I've tasted better.

RAT (*to Badger*) Oughtn't we to *do* something? We're his friends.

BADGER. Yes, you're right. The hour has come.

MOLE (*anxiously—crossing to Badger*) What hour?

BADGER. Whose hour, you should say. Toad's hour. The hour of Toad.

MOLE. Ah! (*He returns to his feast*)

RAT (*quietly*) Well done, Badger. I knew you'd feel that way too.

MOLE (*firmly*) *We'll* teach him to be a sensible Toad.

RAT. How to get him, that's the problem——

BADGER (*gravely*) Let us apply our minds to it.

(*They apply their minds. Absent-mindedly, while thinking,* MOLE *helps himself to beef. Suddenly the bell rings loudly*)

Whoever's that?

(BADGER *shuffles over to the front door* R, *and as he opens it,* TOAD *falls into his arms, panting with fear*)

RAT (*in surprise*) Why, it's Toad!

MOLE. Hallo, Toad, you ought to try some of this beef!

RAT (*fetching the chair* L *of the table and bringing it down* C) Why, what's the matter—Wild-wooders?

(TOAD, *supported by* BADGER, *falls limply into a chair and sits there panting.* MOLE *comes to* R *of him,* RAT *to* L *of him.* BADGER *goes to the front door* R *and closes it*)

TOAD (*warming to it*) An unfortunate breakdown in my car— a loose nut, some trifling mishap—left me stranded at the edge of the wood, far from home.

(BADGER *comes to* RC)

I bethought me of my good friend Mr Badger; he would lend me a sleeping-suit and put me up for the night. As I came whistling through the wood, recking nought of danger, I was suddenly seized upon by a gang of rascally ferrets. I set about them light-heartedly—at the most there were no more than a dozen of them —when suddenly, to my horror, they were reinforced by a posse of scoundrelly weasels. It was then, Ratty—and my dear friend Mole—that I wished I had your assistance. Twelve of the rascals, yes, but twenty-four of them is a different matter. (*He is now standing up, legs straddled, and enjoying himself immensely*) If only you and Mole could have taken a couple of them off my hands, there might have been a different story to tell. As it was, a rear-guard action was forced upon me. Step by step—— (*He realizes a faint hostile something in the air, particularly from the direction of* BADGER. *He goes on less confidently*) Step by step—— (*He looks from one to the other, hoping for a little encouragement, but the atmosphere is now really terrible; nobody could tell even the simplest story in it. He makes a last desperate effort*) Step by step——

BADGER (*solemnly*) Won't you sit down again, Toad?

TOAD (*meekly—sitting again*) Thank you, dear Badger.

RAT. Would you care to be nearer the fire?

TOAD (*faintly*) No, thank you, dear Ratty.

MOLE. Let me put your gloves down for you.

TOAD. It's all right, thank you, dear Mole.

(MOLE *goes back to the table*)

BADGER (*to Rat*) The moment has come, I think, don't you?

RAT. I think so.

BADGER (*to Mole*) You agree?

MOLE. Yes. (*He sighs*)

TOAD (*uneasily*) I say, you fellows, what's all this—— (*He catches* BADGER's *eye and is silent again*)

BADGER (*solemnly*) Toad! I knew your father, worthy animal that he was; I knew your grandfather. It was also my privilege to be slightly acquainted with your uncle, the Archdeacon; of that I shall speak further directly. The question I wish to ask you now is this. At the beginning of the breathless story of adventure to which we have just been listening, you mentioned (*he pauses dramatically*) a motor-car. You implied further that this motor-car had suddenly lost its efficiency. Am I right in supposing that just at this moment your narrative hovered for an instant on the confines of truth?

TOAD (*sulkily*) What do you mean?

RAT. Really, Toad, he couldn't have put it more plainly.

BADGER. I asked you, Toad, if it is indeed a fact that your eighth motor-car is now in as fragmentary a condition as the previous seven?

TOAD (*sulkily*) I had a little accident.

BADGER. Thank you. (*To Rat*) Then I think that in that case we may begin the treatment?

RAT. Yes, I think so.

BADGER (*going up to Mole*) You agree?

MOLE. Yes.

(BADGER *crosses to the fireplace*)

TOAD. I say, you fellows——

(RAT *goes up to Mole.* BADGER *comes down* L)

BADGER. Toad!

(TOAD *looks at him*)

Rise from your chair a moment.

(TOAD *rises*)

Rat.

(RAT *comes down and turns the chair to face* L)

Thank you, Toad!

(BADGER *points to the chair and* TOAD *meekly creeps into it*)

Now then, first of all take those ridiculous goggles off.

TOAD (*plucking up courage*) Shan't! What is the meaning of this gross outrage?

BADGER. Take them off then, you two.

RAT (*as* Toad *looks like showing fight*) It's all for your own good, Toady, old man. (*He removes Toad's goggles, then goes to the fireplace and puts them on the mantelpiece*)

MOLE. It's only because we are so fond of you. (*He puts Toad's gloves on the* L *corner of the table and sits in front of the table*)

BADGER. That is better. It was thus that your father knew you. It was thus that your grandfather, had he survived a year or two longer, would have known you. Now then, Toad. You've disregarded all the warnings we've given you, and you're getting us animals a bad name in the district by your furious driving and your smashes and your rows with the police. I am going to make one more effort to bring you to reason. You will come with me into my study, and there you will hear some facts about yourself. I say the study, because I have decided, for the sake of your revered grandfather, to spare you the pain of a public reproof. Come! (*He crosses to the study door up* RC)

(TOAD *follows him*)

TOAD (*meekly*) Yes, Badger. Thank you, Badger.

(*They go out together*)

RAT (*up* LC) That's no good! Talking to Toad will never cure him. He'll say anything.

MOLE (*crossing to the chair* LC *and putting it back* L *of the table*) Yes. (*He sighs*)

RAT. We must *do* something.

MOLE. Yes. (*He sighs again*)

RAT (*looking at him suddenly*) What's the matter, old fellow? You seem melancholy. Too much beef?

MOLE (*bravely*) Oh, no, it isn't that. It was just—no, never mind, I shall be all right directly. (*He wipes away a tear and sits in the chair* L *of the table*)

RAT. Why, whatever is it?

MOLE. Nothing, Ratty, nothing. I was just admiring Badger's great big house and comparing it with my own little home, which—which I haven't seen lately—just comparing it, you know, and thinking about it—and thinking about it—and comparing it. Not meaning to, you know. Just happening to—think about it.

RAT (*remorsefully*) Oh, Mole!

MOLE (*in a sudden burst*) I know it's a shabby, dingy little place; not like your cosy quarters, or Toad's beautiful Hall, or Badger's great house—but it was my own little home—and I was fond of it—and I went away and forgot all about it—and since we've been down here it's all been coming back to me—perhaps it's the pickles—*I* always had Military Pickles too—I shall be better soon—I don't know what you'll think of me.

RAT (*going to Mole and patting him on the back*) Poor old Mole! Been rather an exciting day, hasn't it? And then the same sort of pickles. (*He goes right round behind the table to front of it and sits on the stool*) Tell me about Mole End. We might go and pay it a visit tomorrow if you've nothing better to do.

MOLE. It wouldn't be fine enough for *you*. You're used to great big places and fine houses. I noticed directly we came in how you stood with your back to the fire so grandly and easily, just as if it were nothing to you.

RAT. Well, *you* tucked into the beef, old chap.

MOLE. Did I?

RAT. Rather! Made yourself quite at home. I said to myself at once, "Mole is used to going out," I said. "Week-end parties at big country houses," I said, "that's nothing to Mole," I said.

MOLE (*eagerly*) Did you really, Ratty?

RAT. Oh, rather! Spotted it at once.

MOLE. Of course there *were* features about Mole End which made it rather—rather——

RAT. Rather a feature?

MOLE. Yes. The statuary. I'd picked up a bit of statuary here and there—you'd hardly think how it livened the place up. Garibaldi, the Infant Samuel, and Queen Victoria—dotted about in odd corners. It had a very pleasing effect, my friends used to tell me.

Rat (*heartily*) I should like to have seen that, Mole, I should indeed. That must have been very striking.

Mole. It was just about now that they used to come carol-singing.

Rat. Garibaldi—and the others?

Mole. The field-mice.

Rat. Oh, yes, of course.

Mole. Quite an institution they were. They never passed me over—always came to Mole End last, and I gave them hot drinks, and supper sometimes, when I could afford it.

Rat. Yes, I remember now hearing about it, and what a fine place Mole End was.

Mole (*wistfully*) Did you? . . . It wasn't very big.

Rat. Between ourselves, I don't much care about these big places. Cosy and tasteful, that's what I always heard about Mole End.

Mole (*squeezing Rat's paw*) You're a good friend, Ratty. I like being with *you*.

Rat. Good old Mole!

No. 10

(*They are happily silent together. Suddenly, faint and far-off and sweet, a carol can be heard* . . . "*the carol that Mr Mole liked*". *They listen raptly*)

(*1st, 4th and 5th verses are sung off* R)

Villagers all, this frosty tide,
Let your door swing open wide,
Though wind may follow, and snow beside,
Yet draw us in by your fire to bide;
Joy shall be yours in the morning,
Joy shall be yours in the morning,
Joy shall be yours in the morning!

Here we stand in the cold and the sleet,
Blowing fingers and stamping feet;
Come from far away you to greet,
You by the fire and we in the street,
Bidding you joy in the morning,
Bidding you joy in the morning,
Bidding you joy in the morning!

For ere one half of the night was gone,
Sudden a star had led us on,
Raining bliss and benison;
Bliss to-morrow and more anon,
Joy for every morning,
Joy for every morning,
Joy for every morning!

Good man Joseph toiled through the snow,
Saw the star o'er the stable low;
Mary she might not further go,
Welcome thatch and litter below!
Joy was hers in the morning,
Joy was hers in the morning,
Joy was hers in the morning!

And then they heard the angels tell
Who were the first to cry Nowell.
Animals all, as it befell,
In the stable where they did dwell;
Joy shall be theirs in the morning,
Joy shall be theirs in the morning,
Joy shall be theirs in the morning!

(*During the carol,* RAT *crosses to the chair* L *of the fireplace, and* MOLE *comes and sits at his feet below him.*

At the end of the first verse a carol-singer enters R. MOLE *gets up and crosses to him, fumbling in his pocket for money. Finding he hasn't any he goes back to* RAT, *who gives him some, and he gives this to the carol-singer, who exits* R.

At the end of the carol the singers cross behind the window C, *and* MOLE *goes up to the window to wish them a merry Christmas, etc. When it is all over they both give a little sigh: for it is now time to get back to business.*

The door of the study opens and BADGER *comes in, leading by the paw a very dejected* TOAD)

BADGER (*kindly*) Sit down there, Toad.

(TOAD *sits down on the chair* L *of the table.* BADGER *goes to the fireplace*)

My friends, I am pleased to inform you that Toad has at last seen the error of his ways. He is truly sorry for his misguided conduct in the past, and he has undertaken to give up motor-cars entirely and for ever in the future. I have his solemn promise to that effect.

MOLE (*eagerly, going to* R *of the table*) Oh, Toad, I *am* glad!
RAT (*doubtfully*) H'm!
BADGER. There is only one thing which remains to be done. Toad, I want you solemnly to repeat before your friends here what you fully admitted to me in the study just now. First, you are sorry for what you have done and see the folly of it all?

(*There is an anxious silence*)

TOAD (*suddenly*) No! I'm *not* sorry. (*He rises and steps forward to* C) And it wasn't folly at all. It was simply glorious!

Badger (RC—*horrified*) What?

Mole (R) Toady!

Rat (*moving down* L) I thought so.

Badger (*going* C *to* Toad) You back-sliding animal, didn't you tell me just now in there——

Toad. Oh yes, yes, in *there.* I'd have said anything in *there.* You're so eloquent, dear Badger, and so moving, and so convincing, and put all your points so frightfully well—you can do what you like with me in *there.* But, thinking it over out *here,* I see that I am not a bit sorry really, so it's no earthly good saying I am; now is it?

Badger. Then you don't promise never to touch a motor-car again?

Toad. Of course I don't. On the contrary, I faithfully promise that the very first motor-car I see (*he crosses* L)—Poop-poop, off I go in it!

Rat (*to Mole*) I told you so.

Badger. Very well, then. Since you won't yield to persuasion, we'll try what force can do. I feared it would come to this all along. You'll stay with me, Toad, until a cure has been effected. My friends, Rat and Mole, will also stay with me and help me to look after you. It's going to be a tedious business, but we will see it out.

No. 10a

Bring him along.

> (Badger *crosses up to* R *of the fireplace, takes down a key from off the wall, then goes over to the door up* RC. Toad *follows, led by* Rat, *but as they get to the door,* Toad *turns and runs down* L. Rat *runs to* L *of him,* Mole *to* R *of him. They catch him and bring him along, and the procession goes slowly, and on* Toad's *part reluctantly, out* RC)

Black Out

Curtain

Scene 3

No. 11

Scene—*Badger's Home on a Spring morning some weeks later.*

Mr Badger *is in the armchair* R *of the fireplace with his feet on another, reading a newspaper, and paying no attention whatever to* Toad, *who is in the paroxysms of another attack.* Toad (*poor fellow*) *has arranged two chairs and a stool with an umbrella through the hole in the middle in a hopeful representation of a motor-car. He sits on the front chair, grasping the umbrella, changing imaginary gears, and making appropriate noises. A sudden (imaginary) block in the traffic pulls him up sharply, though his "Hi, look ahead there!" averts an accident. He gets off and winds up his engine, then lifts the bonnet and peers in. In a little while he is off again; but now a real accident upsets him. The chairs are strewn about and* TOAD *lies panting in the wreckage.* BADGER *lifts an eye, glances at him and goes on with his paper.* MOLE *comes in from the study up* RC. *He looks at Toad.*

MOLE (*up stage* C) Tut-tut! Again?

BADGER (*still reading his paper*) The third crash this morning. There seems to be a good deal of traffic on the road today.

MOLE. Poor old Toad!

BADGER. I always warned you, my dear Mole, that in these cases the poison takes a long time to work itself out of the system. But we're improving; we're improving daily. Let me see. It's Rat's turn to be on guard this morning, isn't it?

MOLE. Yes. (*He helps* TOAD *to the bed* L) Lean on me, old fellow. That's right. Lie down a bit. (*Business with bed-clothes*) You'll be better directly. I daresay Rat will read to you, if you ask him. (*He puts the umbrella against the flat,* R *of the fireplace, and replaces the chairs at the table* C. *The stool is left* C)

TOAD (*weakly*) Thank you, my dear friend, thank you. Don't let me be a burden to you.

MOLE. That's all right, Toady. We'll soon get you well.

BADGER (*rising and coming down to Mole* C) What do you say to a bit of a ramble along the hedgerows, Mole. And there's a new burrow I want to show you. I must say I like being out in this sort of weather.

MOLE (*eagerly*) Just what I was about to suggest. I wish old Ratty could come too. I suppose—— (*He looks across at Toad*)

BADGER. No, no, it wouldn't be safe. (*In a whisper*) Toad's quiet now, and when he is quiet, then he's at his artfullest. (*He crosses* R) I know him.

MOLE. Yes, I suppose so. But it's such an exciting sort of day. Rat would love it so.

(RAT *enters through the study door, and goes above the table* C, *upon which is a bowl of potatoes with a knife*)

RAT. Hallo, you fellows, not off yet?

BADGER. Just going. (*He goes to the door* R) Toad's quiet now. But keep an eye on him. I don't trust him.

RAT. That's all right.

MOLE (*quietly to Rat*) I believe he's worse than Badger thinks. Look after him well, poor old Toad.

RAT. That's all right. (*He moves down to the stool* C, *and puts the bowl and knife on the stool*)

BADGER (*at the door*) Coming, Mole?

MOLE. Coming. Poor old Ratty, it is a shame being kept in like this.

(BADGER *goes out* R)

Still, we all have our turns.

RAT. Of course we do. Good luck to you.

MOLE. Good-bye!

BADGER (*off*) Are you coming, Mole?

MOLE (*going to the door* R, *then crossing back to Rat, then over to Toad*). Coming! Good-bye! Good-bye, Toad!

TOAD (*faintly*) Good-bye, dear old Mole.

BADGER (*appearing at the door again*) Mole!

MOLE (*ecstatically*) What a morning! I don't think I ever remember——

BADGER (*severely*) When I was young, we *always* had mornings like this.

(*They go out by the door* R)

RAT (*moving the stool nearer to Toad and commencing to peel the potatoes*) Now, old boy, we're going to have a jolly morning together, so jump up, and I'll do my best to amuse you.

TOAD. Dear, kind Rat, how little you realize my condition, and how very far I am from jumping up now—if ever. But do not trouble about me. I hate being a burden to my friends, and I do not expect to be one much longer.

RAT. Well, I hope not too. You've been a fine bother to us all *this* time, you have really, Toad. Weeks and weeks! And now, in weather like this, and the boating season just beginning! It's too bad of you!

TOAD. I'm a nuisance to my friends, I know, I know.

RAT (*wistfully*) I was thinking about my river yesterday evening, and I—I wrote a little poem. (*Shyly*) Do you think you would like to hear it?

TOAD. As you will, my dear Ratty. It may comfort my last hours.

RAT (*eagerly*) It's about the ducks. I used to have such fun with them. You know when they stand on their heads suddenly, well, then I dive down and tickle their necks, and they come up all spluttering and angry, and shaking their feathers at me—of course they aren't angry really, because it's all fun—and then I used to sit on the bank in the sun, and pretend I was coming in after 'em again, and—— (*He breaks off suddenly and announces*) "Ducks' Ditty."

No. 12

All along the backwater,
Through the rushes tall,
Ducks are a-dabbling,
Up tails all!

Ducks' tails, drakes' tails,
Yellow feet aquiver,
Yellow bills all out of sight
Busy in the river!

Every one for what he likes!
We like to be
Heads down, tails up,
Dabbling free!

High in the blue above
Swifts whirl and call—
We are down a-dabbling—
Up tails all!

(*He looks in front of him, seeing it all*)

TOAD (*with a deep sigh*) Thank you. I am glad to have heard it. . . . Ratty?

RAT (*waking from his reverie*) Yes?

TOAD. I wonder if I could bother you—but no, you have been too kind already.

RAT. Why, what is it? You know we'd do anything for you, all of us.

TOAD. Then could I beg you, for the last time probably, to step round to the village as quickly as possible—even now it may be too late—and fetch the doctor? (*He groans*)

RAT. But what do you want a doctor for?

TOAD. Surely you have noticed—— But no, why should you? Noticing things is only a trouble. Tomorrow, indeed, you may be saying to yourself, "Oh, if only I had noticed sooner! If only I had *done* something! Too late, too late!" . . . Forget that I asked. Naturally you want to go on with your poetry. Have you ever done anything in the way of epitaphs?

RAT (*alarmed*) Look here, old man, of course I'll fetch a doctor to you, if you really want one. But it hasn't come to that yet. You're imagining. Now let's talk about something more cheerful.

TOAD (*with an angelic expression*) I fear, dear friend, that talk can do little in a case like this—or doctors either, for that matter. Still, one must grasp at the slightest straw. And by the way—while you are in the village—I hate to bother you, but I fancy that you pass the door—*would* you mind asking my lawyer to step up? (*He closes his eyes*)

RAT (*rising and taking the bowl to the table*) A lawyer! He *must* be bad. (*Aloud*) All right, Toad, I'll go. (*He makes his preparations to go out, glancing from time to time at the unconscious Toad as he does so. Then a brilliant idea occurs to him*)

RAT (RC—*loudly*) I'm going now, Toad. (*He goes to the door* R *and takes the key out of the lock*)

TOAD (*faintly, his eyes closed*) Thank you, thank you!

RAT (*moving back to* RC) I'll bring the doctor and the lawyer, and we'll be back as quickly as we can.

TOAD. You're a good fellow, Ratty.

RAT. Good-bye, old boy. Keep your spirits up.

TOAD. Good-bye!

(*Humming a tune and making a good deal of noise,* RAT *goes out. Then very quietly he steals back again and peers round the door.* TOAD *is apparently still on the verge of dissolution.* RAT *nods to himself in satisfaction with his strategy; Toad's illness is obviously genuine. We hear him as he starts through the Wild Wood, singing "Ducks' Ditty" to himself. As the song dies in the distance,* TOAD *opens an eye. Then the other eye. He raises his head and listens. He sits up in bed, still listening. Then with a laugh he jumps up and takes the floor*)

TOAD (*boastfully*) Ha, ha, ha! Smart piece of work that! (*He chatters to himself as he collects his coat, gloves, goggles, and other accessories of outdoor life*) Brain against brute force—and brain came out on the top—as it's bound to do. Poor old Ratty! My! Won't he catch it when Badger gets back! A worthy fellow, Ratty, with many good qualities, but absolutely no finesse. I must take him in hand some day, and see if I can make something of him.

No. 13

(*He is ready now; as he goes to the door* L *he begins to sing*)

The world has held great heroes,
As history-books have showed;
But never a name to go down to fame
Compared with that of Toad!

(TOAD *is singing the last line as he opens the door. Then with a triumphant* "Poop-poop! Poop-poop!" *he disappears*)

CURTAIN

ACT III

SCENE I

No. 14

SCENE—*The Court-House.*

> *A bare, clean, whitewashed room, furnished with a Bench, a Jury-box, and a little extra space for the witnesses and spectators. (See Photograph of Scene)*

It is crowded today, for the notorious TOAD *is to be tried, and there is every prospect that he will be sentenced to a severe term of penal servitude. In the corner down* R, *sitting gloomily together on a stone slab, are* BADGER *and* RAT. MOLE *is seated on the floor* R *of them. On the Bench up* L, *where the Judge is supposed to sit, is* TOAD, *a handkerchief covering his face. After a little while the Jury enter down* R, *and cross over* L *to the Jury-box, and a* TURKEY, *a* DUCK, *four* SQUIRRELS, *five* RABBITS *and the* CHIEF WEASEL *all crowd together. An* USHER, *tall and thin, wanders round the room with a list in his hand, ticking off those present.*

USHER (C) One Judge. (*He looks at the Bench and marks off what he believes to be the Judge on his list*) Twelve Jury. (*He counts them and marks them off*) One policeman witness. (*To the* POLICEMAN *who is standing* R) That's you. (*As the* POLICEMAN *is about to step forward*) Now, don't you go a-moving or you'll muddle me. One policeman—and one prisoner. (*He looks at the Dock up* R, *by the side of which is a* GAOLER) Hallo! That's funny. Where is the prisoner? (*He moves down* L)

POLICEMAN (*staggered*) Well, I know I brought him in. (*Loudly*) Toad! Where are you?

(*The* GAOLER *looks around*)

TOAD (*looking up from the Bench, sadly*) Here I am.

USHER (*going up to* L *of the Bench*) What yer doing there? Come down out of it!

(*The* POLICEMAN *goes to* R *of the Bench. The* GAOLER *to* R *of the* POLICEMAN)

TOAD (*meekly*) I thought this was where the prisoners went.

(*The* GAOLER *puts* TOAD *in the Dock, then moves round to* R *of it. The* POLICEMAN *goes to* L *of the Dock. The* USHER *to* LC)

EVERYBODY. Did you hear what he said . . . What was it? . . . Well, of all the cheek . . . Just like Toad . . . What was it? I didn't hear . . .

34

(*All rise as the* JUDGE *enters* R *and goes to his seat up* C. *When he is seated they all sit again. The* JUDGE *snaps his fingers for tea, and everybody looks round saying tea.* TOAD *has his tea, and he passes it to the* POLICEMAN, *who gives it to the* JUDGE. *The* JUDGE *drinks his tea, then passes it back to the* POLICEMAN, *who passes it on to the* GAOLER, *who takes it off stage down* R, *afterwards returning to his original position*)

USHER (*stepping forward*) Silence!
EVERYBODY (*to everybody else*) Silence! Silence! . . .
JUDGE (*annoyed*) Stop saying "Silence!"
EVERYBODY (*to everybody else*) Stop saying "Silence".
JUDGE. It's worse than ever! (*To the Usher*) Try them with "Hush".
USHER (*in a loud whisper*) Hush!

(*Everybody hushes*)

JUDGE. Please understand, once and for all, that unless I have complete hush, it will be impossible for the prisoner to be tried.
TOAD. I don't want to be tried.
JUDGE (*sternly*) Impossible for him to be tried, but not impossible for him to be severely sentenced.
BADGER (*in tears*) Alack! Alack! Oh hapless Toad!
TOAD. Well, it was fun anyway.
USHER. Oyes, oyes, oyes! The Court being now open, his lordship will deliver his usual song to the Jury.

No. 14a

(*The Judge's song*)

If an animal errs or a citizen sins,
Whether rabbit or weasel or ferret, he
Is certain as soon as the trial begins
That I'll polish him off with celerity.
And I always come down like a cart-load of bricks
On Toads—on Toads and their tricks.

(*Here the* USHER *takes a step forward*)

JUDGE (*hastily*) There's another verse.

My methods are quick, and my eye's on the clock
To avoid the delay which a Jury hates,
Especially so when a Toad's in the dock,
For there's something in Toads which infuriates.
So I always come down like a truck-load of coal
On Toads—on Toads-in-a-hole, Toads-in-a-hole.

(*Near the end of the second verse, the* POLICEMAN *applauds, but the* JUDGE *stops him. On the low note all lean forward, then back again on completion of the note*)

JUDGE (*clearing his throat*) H'm! Friends and fellow-citizens! We see before us, cowering in the Dock—— We do not see before us, cowering in the Dock——

(*The* POLICEMAN *and the* GAOLER *look at the Dock.* TOAD, *who has been crouching down, appears*)

We see before us, cowering in the Dock, one of the most notorious and hardened malefactors of our time, the indigenous Toad.

TOAD. I'm not indigenous.

JUDGE (*grimly*) Well, if you're not, you very soon will be. We see before us, I say, this monster of iniquity, and it is our duty to try him fairly and without prejudice, and to sentence him to the very sharpest term of imprisonment that we can think of, so as to learn him not to do it again. We shall then adjourn for lunch.

(*Cries of* "Hear, hear!" *The* USHER *puts his thumbs up to the Jury*)

It may be that after lunch we shall see things in a more rosy light, and be tempted to dilute justice with mercy, to the extent of re-mitting some thirty or forty years of the sentence. If so, we shall fight against the temptation. If, on the other hand, we see things in a more sombre light, and realize suddenly that we have been too lenient with the cowering criminal before us, we shall not hesitate to remedy our error. (*Kindly*) Has the prisoner anything to say before we pass on?

TOAD (*meekly*) No.

JUDGE. Very well. Then I proceed to the charge. The counts against the prisoner are as follows. (*To the Usher*) By the way, is the Jury all present? I particularly want the Jury to hear this. Just call 'em out and see.

USHER. Certainly, m'lord. (*Coming down* LC) Mr Turkey.

TURKEY. Gobble! Gobble!

USHER. Mr Duck.

DUCK. Quack! Quack!

USHER. Four squirrels!

SQUIRRELS. Here!

USHER. Six rabbits!

RABBITS. Here!

(RAT *rises and holds up his hand*)

RAT (*firmly*) I object.

(*Sensation*)

JUDGE (*putting on his glasses*) What's the matter? (*He rises and comes down* RC) Who is it? What did he—— Ah, Ratty, my little friend, is it you? (*He shakes hands with Rat*) Delighted to see you. If you will just wait until I have got this ruffian off my hands, we can have a little talk.

(*The* Usher *moves towards the Judge*)

What about lunching with me? (*To the Usher*) Go on, please.

(*The* Usher *moves back to* lc)

Usher. Six rabbits!
Rabbits. Here!
Rat. I object, my lord.
Judge (*surprised*) Object?
Rat. One of the rabbits is a weasel.
Chief Weasel (*indignantly, rising*) I'm not! I'm a rabbit.
Rat. He's a weasel.
Judge. Dear, dear! A difference of opinion. (*To the Usher*)
What are we to do? What *does* one do?
Usher. He *says* he's a rabbit, my lord, and he ought to know.

(Chief Weasel *sits*)

Judge (*to Rat*) There's something in that. You can't make a
mistake about a thing of that sort.
Rat (*doggedly*) He's a weasel.
Chief Weasel. I'm not!
Rat. That proves it. (*To Weasel*) Why should you say you
aren't, if you aren't?
Judge. But of course he says he aren't if he aren't. I mean *if*
he aren't, then he aren't, so naturally he says he aren't. (*He fans
himself with his handkerchief*)
Rat. But he wouldn't *say* he wasn't, if he wasn't. The other
rabbits didn't say they wasn't. Why didn't they say they wasn't?
Because they aren't.
Judge (*to the Usher*) Just make a note that if this goes on I shall
want a glass of iced water.
Rat (*eagerly*) Of course if you aren't, you don't say you aren't,
but if you weren't, you would say you were.
Judge (*completely muddled*) But you wouldn't say you aren't, if
you weren't, and on the other hand—— (*Despairingly*) I think
we'd better begin this trial *all* over again.

(*Sighs from everybody*)

Usher. Yes, my lord. Much the best way.
Judge (*to Rat*) You can tell me your objections afterwards,
when we have this desperate ruffian safely lodged in a dungeon.
Rat. He's a weasel! I know he's a weasel! You can see he's a
weasel! It isn't fair!
Judge (*soothingly*) There, there, there! We'll talk about it
calmly at lunch. There's a nice saddle of mutton—and red-
currant jelly. (*He goes back to his seat*)
Mole (*boldly, rising*) It's a shame, that's what it is, when everybody knows what the weasels are. (*He sits down again*)

CHIEF WEASEL (*to the Rabbits, rising*) I'm a rabbit, aren't I a rabbit? (*Under his breath*) Say I am, quick!

RABBITS (*terrified*) Y-yes.

CHIEF WEASEL. There you are. Naturally there are lots of different kinds of rabbit, and I'm one of the different kinds.

RAT. No, you're not. (*He sits*)

CHIEF WEASEL. Yes, I am. (*He also sits*)

JUDGE. Please, please! For *my* sake. (*To the Usher*) Now then, *all* over again.

USHER (*stolidly*) Mr Turkey.

TURKEY. Gobble! Gobble!

USHER. Mr Duck.

DUCK. Quack! Quack!

USHER. Four squirrels.

SQUIRRELS. Here!

USHER. Five ordinary rabbits.

RABBITS. Here!

USHER. One different kind of rabbit.

CHIEF WEASEL. Here!

USHER. That's the lot, my lord.

ALFRED (*suddenly appearing from* R, *and going round* C *to* L *of the Judge*) What about me?

JUDGE (*putting on his glasses*) What *is* this?

ALFRED (*in the Usher's voice*) Alfred! (*Squeakily*) Here!

JUDGE (*to the Policeman*) Lead it out.

ALFRED (*as he is led out* R, *by the Policeman*) All right, all right. I only wanted to help. No *esprit de corps*. That's what's the matter with them all. No *esprit de corps*.

(*They go out* R)

JUDGE. Now then. (*Looking at his watch*) We haven't too much time. Did I sing you that little song of mine?

(*The* USHER *nods "yes" and gives a paper to the Judge*)

The counts against the prisoner are as follows: First, that he did maliciously steal a valuable motor-car without so much as a "with your leave" or a "by your leave". Second, that being in the said motor-car, he did drive recklessly and to the common danger. Third, that on being apprehended he was guilty of gross impertinence to the rural police. (*Cheerfully*) Now then, Toad, what have you got to say about all that?

TOAD. I wasn't driving recklessly. I was just going along quietly at about seventy miles an hour, when I saw a policeman in front of me. Naturally I quickened up to see if he wanted anything. Same as anyone else would have done who's fond of policemen.

POLICEMAN (*who has returned*) Recklessly *and* to the common danger.

TOAD. Rubbish!

POLICEMAN. And what did you call me, eh?

TOAD. How can I remember? Officer, constable, sergeant——

POLICEMAN. No, you didn't.

JUDGE. Now we're getting at it. What did he call you?

POLICEMAN (*annoyed*) He called me fat-face.

(*Sensation*)

JUDGE (*aghast*) Fat-face!

EVERYBODY (*to everybody else*) He called him fat-face!

JUDGE. This is terrible. This adds years to my life. (*To the Policeman*) You mean to tell me that this ruffian, this incorrigible rogue whom I am about to sentence to a severe term of penal servitude, had the audacity to call a representative of the Law "fat-face"?

RAT. Oh, Toady!

JUDGE. Fat-face! Did I hear it aright? Fat-face?

POLICEMAN (*sulkily*) We don't want to make a song about it. I told you what he called me, and that's what he called me.

USHER (*stolidly*) Fat-face.

TOAD. I didn't mean *him* any more than anyone else. I just murmured the expression to myself. It's a way I have. I'm that sort of person. I murmur things to myself.

USHER. He admits that he passed the expression "fat-face", my lord, and that's good enough for any ordinary jury.

CHIEF WEASEL (*rising*) Speaking as a special kind of rabbit, I say that it's good enough for *me*.

MOLE (*rising*) Weasel! (*He sits again*)

CHIEF WEASEL (*sitting*) Shut up!

JUDGE. Very well. We have the prisoner condemned out of his own mouth of using most frightful cheek to a member of the rural police. We shall now sentence him severely.

EVERYBODY. Oh! oh!

USHER. Wait a bit, my lord. There's that little matter of stealing a valuable motor-car without so much as a "with your leave" or a "by your leave".

JUDGE. Does it matter? I mean compared with this unspeakable impertinence to which the prisoner has already confessed?

USHER. Well, it adds more to the sentence, like.

JUDGE. Ah, well, in that case we must certainly go into the matter. Well, Toad, what have you got to say about *that*?

TOAD. I didn't mean to steal it. It was this way. I was just having a bit of lunch at an inn. I had been very ill—hadn't I, Ratty?

(RAT *rises and says* "Yes")

—and my dear friends Mr Rat and Mr Mole and Mr Badger had been looking after me.

(*The three friends rise and all talk at once, but at a* "Hush!" *from the* JUDGE *they stop immediately and sit down again*)

It was the first time I'd been up and out, and I was having my bit of lunch—just a round of beef and a few pickled walnuts and a couple of helpings of treacle pudding—when I heard outside "Poop-poop, poop-poop!"

JUDGE. You heard *what?*

TOAD (*raptly*) Poop-poop, poop-poop!

USHER (*stolidly*) Imitation of motor-car.

JUDGE. Oh! (*To himself*) Poop-poop! Poop-poop! (*He shakes his head*) No, I don't seem to get it.

TOAD. Well, then two gentlemen came in to lunch, and as soon as I'd finished mine, I went out to look at their car. I thought there couldn't be any harm in my only just *looking* at it. So I looked at it. And then naturally I began to say to myself, "I wonder if this car *starts* easily." So I wound it up just to see. And then naturally I stepped into the driver's seat, just as I always do, and . . . and then I saw a policeman with a very fat fa—with a very nice expression, a very *handsome* policeman, and he said, "You're going a hundred and seventy miles an hour," and I said, "Of course if you say so, dear Mr Policeman," and then——

JUDGE (*to the Usher*) All this makes it worse, doesn't it?

USHER. Much worse.

JUDGE (*relieved*) I thought so. It means we can give him a stiffer sentence?

USHER. A much stiffer one.

JUDGE. Good. You were saying, Toad?

BADGER (*rising weightily*) May *I* say a few words now, my lord?

(*He crosses to* LC *and faces the Judge*)

JUDGE. Who is this?

USHER. Mr Badger, a well-known and highly respected member of the community.

JUDGE. So it is, so it is. Well, Mr Badger?

BADGER. Alack! Alack! O, hapless Toad! O, ill-fated animal.

JUDGE (*to the Usher*) Is it a recitation?

BADGER. I knew his father, I knew his grandfather, I knew his uncle, the Archdeacon.

JUDGE. This makes it very serious indeed.

BADGER. Many an afternoon have I spent in communion with his father at Toad Hall—one of the most attractive riverside residences with carriage-sweep.

JUDGE. Dear, dear! *With* carriage-sweep, you say?

BADGER. Unhappy day! O, feckless Toad! O, rash and ill-advised animal! (*He goes back to the slab, sits and breaks down*)

(RAT *and* MOLE *console him*)

JUDGE. It was a recitation, most interesting. We are all indebted to Mr Badger for his profound and helpful observations. Now, I think, we can proceed to business.

CHIEF WEASEL. Guilty!

JUDGE. Of course he's guilty. Mr Usher, will you please tell us what is the very stiffest penalty we can impose for each of the three offences for which the prisoner stands convicted? Without, of course, giving him the benefit of the doubt, because there isn't any.

USHER. Well, my lord, suppose you were to say a year for the theft, which is mild, and three years for the furious driving, which is lenient, and fifteen years for the cheek, which is purely nominal; those figures, if added together correctly, tot up to nineteen years——

JUDGE. First-rate!

USHER. So you'd better make it a round twenty and be on the safe side.

TOAD (*meekly*) I don't mind if it isn't quite round.

JUDGE. Silence! An excellent suggestion, Mr Usher. Now, prisoner, pull yourself together and try and stand up straight. It's going to be twenty years for you this time. And mind, if you appear before us again, on any charge whatever, we shall have to deal with you very seriously.

CHIEF WEASEL. Hear, hear!

MOLE. Shut up!

JUDGE. Twenty years. Don't forget. Now then, prisoner, before the rest of us adjourn for lunch, is there anything you would like to say in the nature of a farewell speech? Any last words or vale-dictory utterances?

TOAD (*boldly*) Yes.

JUDGE (*kindly*) Well, well, what is it?

TOAD. Fat-face!

JUDGE (*aghast*) Fat-face? *Me?*

TOAD (*wildly*) All of you! All the whole lot of you! All fat-faces! (*He steps out of the Dock to* C) I am Toad, the Terror of the Highway (*to the Jury*), Toad, the Traffic-queller, the Lord of the Lone Trail (*he turns* R *and goes up to the Judge*), before whom all must give way or be smitten into nothingness and everlasting night. (*He moves down* L) I am the Toad, the handsome, the popular, the successful Toad. (*He turns to the court*)

    (*The* POLICEMAN *goes to* C, *and the* GAOLER *to down* R)

And what are you? Just fat-faces.

JUDGE. Well, of all the ungrateful things to say!

TOAD. I am the great, the magnificent, the incomprehensible Toad! (*He creeps up to the Judge*)

    (*The* POLICEMAN *and the* GAOLER *go up stage and meet* L *of the Dock*)

JUDGE. To call *me*, after all I've done for him, fat-face!

Toad. The great Toad!

Rat (*sadly*) Oh, Toady, boasting again!

(Badger, Rat *and* Mole *go off* R)

No. 15.

(Toad *breaks into his chant*)

> The world has held great heroes,
> As history-books have showed;

(*The* Judge *comes down* RC. *The* Usher *moves over to the Jury-box*)

> But never a name to go down to fame
> Compared with that of Toad!

(Toad *scatters the* Jury *and the* Usher *is knocked down*)

Judge. Silence!

Toad. The clever men at Oxford

(*He moves towards the* Judge, *who goes behind the Dock*)

> Know all there is to be knowed,
> But they none of them know one half as much
> As intelligent, Mr Toad!

Judge. Stop him, somebody! Stop him!

Toad. The Army all saluted,
> As they marched along the road;

(*Some of the* Jury *go off* L. *The* Usher *tries to crawl off down* R)

> Was it the King? or Fat-face?
> No. (*With his foot on the Usher's back*) It was Mr Toad!

(*The* Policeman *and the* Gaoler *come down and hold him. The* Usher *escapes off* R)

Chief Weasel. Now then! Now then! Better come quietly!

(Chief Weasel *exits* L)

Toad (*as he is hustled away*) The Queen and her ladies-in-waiting
> Sat in the window and sewed:
> She cried "Look! who's that *handsome* man?"
> They answered, "Mr Toad."

(Toad's *voice is heard more and more faintly in the distance, as he is led to the dungeon.*
All exit off R *except the* Judge)

> Mr Toad! Mr Toad! Mr Toad!

Black Out

Curtain

Scene 2

No. 16.

Scene—*A Dungeon.* (*See Photograph of Scene*)

On a piece of sacking in the c Toad *sleeps uneasily. The door* l *is un-locked, and* Phoebe, *the gaoler's daughter, comes dancing in with a menu. She then goes out, and after a very short while returns with a tray on which there is a glass of water and a crust of bread. She does not seem to think that this will satisfy* Toad, *for after giving him one or two quizzical looks, she removes the tray with this unwholesome fare and enters this time with a tray on which there is a cup of tea and hot-buttered toast. This she places on the table* c. *At the end of the dance* Toad *sits up and takes notice.*

Phoebe. Good morning, Toad.

Toad (*gloomily*) Good morning, woman.

Phoebe (l *of Toad*) Slept well?

Toad. Slept well? How could I sleep well, immured in a dark and noisome dungeon like this?

Phoebe. Well, some do . . . See, I've brought your breakfast.

Toad. Then you will oblige me by taking it away again.

Phoebe. What—aren't you ever going to eat any more?

Toad. You don't understand. This is the end.

Phoebe. You've said that every day for a month past. The end of what?

Toad. The end of everything. At least it is the end of the career of Toad, which is the same thing. (*He paces up and down*)

Phoebe (r *of the table, arranging the breakfast*) Nice hot-buttered toast and tea.

Toad (*coming to below the table*) Oh, despairing and—— Did you say *hot*-buttered toast?

Phoebe (*crossing above the table to* l *of it*) Made it myself, I did.

Toad (*his mouth full of it, crossing to down* l) Believe me, girl, I am not ungrateful. You must pay me a visit at Toad Hall one of these days. Drop in to tea one afternoon.

Phoebe. Is that where you live?

Toad (*nodding*) Finest house in these parts for miles around.

Phoebe. You're feeling better, aren't you?

Toad. The artistic temperament. We have our ups and downs. (*He returns to his breakfast,* r *of the table*)

Phoebe (*looking at him thoughtfully*) Now I wonder.

Toad (*casually*) Any prisoners ever been known to escape from this castle of yours?

Phoebe. Never.

Toad (*a little dashed*) Oh! . . . Well, I must see what I can do. I must give my mind to it one day. Excellent buttered toast this.

Phoebe. *I've* been giving my mind to it lately.

TOAD. That's the only way to make really good toast.

PHOEBE. I didn't mean to that. I meant to escaping. I think I see a way in which you might do it.

TOAD (*dropping his toast in his excitement*) You're going to help me? (*He goes to* C *below the table*)

PHOEBE (*going to Toad*) Yes. I like you, Toad, and I've felt sorry for you, and for your friends, who want to see you again so badly. And I think it's a shame the way you've been treated.

TOAD. They were afraid of me, that's what it was. (*He puffs out his cheeks*)

PHOEBE. Now listen. I have an aunt who is a washerwoman.

TOAD (*kindly*) There, there! Never mind. Think no more about it. I have several aunts who *ought* to be washerwomen.

PHOEBE. Do be quiet a minute, Toad. You talk too much, that's your chief fault. Now my aunt does the washing for all the prisoners in the castle. Naturally we keep anything of that sort in the family. She brings the washing back Friday morning—that's today. Now you're very rich—at least you're always telling me so —and for a few pounds I think I could persuade her to lend you her dress and bonnet and so on, and you could escape as the castle washerwoman. You're very much alike in some ways— particularly about the figure.

TOAD (*indignantly*) We're *not*! (*He crosses to down* L) I have a very elegant figure—for what I am.

PHOEBE. So has my aunt—for what *she* is. But have it your own way, you horrid proud ungrateful animal, when I'm trying to help you!

TOAD (*quickly*) Yes, yes, that's all right, thank you very much indeed. (*He moves back to* C *and turns to* PHOEBE, *who is now up stage* LC) But I was only thinking—— You surely wouldn't have Mr Toad, of Toad Hall, going about the country disguised as a washerwoman?

PHOEBE. All right, then you can stop here as a Toad. I suppose you want to go off in a coach-and-four?

TOAD (*moving up to Phoebe*) No, no! Please! You are a good, kind, clever girl, and I am indeed a proud and stupid Toad. Introduce me to your worthy aunt, if you will be so kind. It would be a privilege to meet her.

PHOEBE. That's better. (*As she goes out*) With a little trouble you'd make quite a nice Toad.

(PHOEBE *exits* L)

TOAD (*as the door closes*) Chit! (*He bursts happily into song again as he gets the stool from* L *of the table and puts it at* R *of the table. He then arranges a little collection of money on the table, in such a way that it looks like an accident rather than a bribe. When satisfied, he fetches the chair from up* LC, *and brings it to* L *of the table, then moves above the table to* R *of it*)

(PHOEBE *enters* L *with her* AUNT, *who appears to be dressed in a blanket. She has a bundle of clothes under her arm. They both come to* C)

PHOEBE. This is Mr Toad. My aunt.

AUNT. Good morning.

TOAD (*in his society manner*) Good morning, dear lady. Charming weather we are having, are we not? Pray sit down.

(AUNT *sits* L *of the table.* PHOEBE *remains standing* L *of her*)

Your niece tells me that you—er—attend to the—er—that is, you have under your charge the habiliments, the more mutable habiliments of the inhabitants of the castle.

AUNT (*to Toad*) I wash.

TOAD. Quite so, quite so.

PHOEBE. I told you the idea, Aunt, didn't I?

AUNT (*eyeing the money*) Some of it.

(*There is an awkward silence.* PHOEBE *catches* TOAD's *eye and indicates the money*)

TOAD. Quite so. (*He clears his throat loudly*) I was wondering—naturally I shouldn't want to carry all my money about with me —indeed, in the costume suggested (*he indicates the bundle of clothes*) —I wondered if you would oblige me so far—purely as a favour to *me*——

AUNT. Is that the money?

TOAD (*indicating the money on the table*) Just a little—er—I haven't counted it——

AUNT. I have.

TOAD. Oh! . . . Well?

AUNT. Here you are. (*She rises and hands over her bundle—cotton print gown, apron, shawl and rusty black bonnet*)

TOAD (*seizing the bundle*) My dear lady, I am eternally your debtor. Should you ever find yourself in the neighbourhood of Toad Hall, a visit, whether professional or social—— (*He holds up the dress*) Er—how do I——

PHOEBE (*much amused*) I'll help you.

AUNT. You told him the condition?

TOAD. Condition?

PHOEBE. My aunt thinks she ought to be gagged and bound, so as to look as if she had been overcome. You'd like it, too. You wanted to leave the prison in style.

TOAD (*beamingly*) An excellent idea. So much more in keeping with my character.

AUNT. I brought a bit of rope along, in case like.

TOAD. Splendid!

AUNT (*enjoying it*) Got a nankerchief?

TOAD (*producing one*) Yes.

AUNT. Then you gags me first. (*In a hoarse whisper*) Help! Help! Help! Help! Help!

Toad (*carried away by the realism of this*) Silence, woman, else I gag thee!

Aunt (*undeterred*) Help! Help! Help!

Toad (*advancing with the gag*) Thou hast brought it on thyself. (*He gags her*)

Aunt (*pulling down the gag*) A little tighter, I think. . . . Help! Help! Help!

Toad (*pulling it tighter*) A murrain on thy cackling tongue! There! (*To Phoebe*) Now then, lend a hand with this rope. (*He is R of the chair*)

Phoebe. How brave you are! (*She comes to L of the chair and helps him*)

Toad (*regarding the Aunt with pride*) A neat bit of work that. (*He goes C*) Now then, how do I get into this? (*He holds up the dress in front of him*)

Phoebe. Silly, not like that. Here, give it to me . . . Now then. (*She helps Toad in, and does him up*) Apron . . . Shawl . . . Now the bonnet. There! Well, upon my word, you're the very living image of her!

(*The* Aunt *makes frantic indications of a desire to speak*)

Toad. What's the matter with her?

Phoebe (*moving up to R of Aunt*) She wants to say something, I think. (*She takes off the gag*)

Aunt (*with conviction*) Too ugly.

Phoebe. Who is?

Aunt. He is.

Toad. My good woman——

Aunt. Much too ugly. Never do at all.

Toad (*amazed*) Really——

Aunt. Not a bit like me. Not good-looking enough.

Toad (*going to L of the chair*) Here, give me the gag!

Aunt. Not *nearly* good-looking enough. Not—— (*But she is gagged again*)

Phoebe (*crossing L*) Now then, Toad, we must hurry. I'll take you to the end of the corridor, and then you go straight down the stairs—you can't mistake the way—and if any of the gaolers stop you and chaff you a bit—because she's very popular, Aunt is——

Toad (*coldly*) I shouldn't have thought it.

Phoebe. Then you must give them a bit of chaff back, but respectable, of course, being a widow woman with a character to lose.

No. 17

Now good-bye and good luck.

Toad (*nervously*) Good-bye, good-bye. If you're ever in the neighbourhood of Toad Hall——

Phoebe. Which I shan't be. Now, come on, there's a good

Toad. You can thank me when you've escaped. Now, don't forget—you're a washerwoman. (*She leads the way out*)

TOAD. Yes, yes, we must be off. (*Nervously*) I wish I knew a
little more what washerwomen talked about. (*In a falsetto voice, as
he goes out* L *with Phoebe*) I remember once when I was ironing a
shirt-front——

Black Out

CURTAIN

SCENE 3

No. 18

SCENE—*The Canal Bank. Early morning.*
> *A quiet spot by the canal bank. The tow-path cuts along by the edge
> of a wood, in which, just here, is a little clearing. (See Photograph of
> Scene)*

At the entrance, half in, half out of a big hollow tree LC, *lies a heap of old
clothing: discarded, it would seem, by some washerwoman. A* WHITE
RABBIT *comes in* L, *does a dance, then goes off again* R. *The clothing
moves. Evidently there is a washerwoman inside it. A voice comes from
the interior. It is our friend* TOAD.

TOAD (*sleepily*) I'll wear the light brown suit, and tell the car
to be round at eleven o'clock . . . No, leave the blinds down. (*He
sleeps again*)

> (*Two baby* RABBITS *come by with their* MAMA, *on their way to
> school. They cross from* L *to* R)

FIRST BABY RABBIT (*Harold,* L *of the tree*) What's 'at? (*He gazes
at Toad*)

MAMA RABBIT (C) Now, now, come along, Harold, you'll be
late for school.

SECOND BABY RABBIT (*Lucy*) What's Harold doing? (*She is* R *of
Mama*)

HAROLD (*rooted to the hollow tree*) What is it?

MAMA RABBIT. Never mind now. Just some poor old washerwoman taking a rest. Come along, there's a good boy.

HAROLD. May I play with it? (*He goes to* R *of the tree*)

MAMA RABBIT. After school, perhaps.

LUCY (*primly*) I like school. (*With an insufferable air of know-
ledge*) Twice two are four, twice three are six——

HAROLD. May I play with it now?

MAMA RABBIT. Not now, dear.

LUCY. What's Harold saying?

HAROLD. Do washerwomans know tables?

MAMA RABBIT. I expect they do. (*She crosses* R)

LUCY (*proudly*) I know my twice times. Twice two are four,
twice three are six——

HAROLD. What are washerwomans for?

MAMA RABBIT. Now, now, come along. (*She goes to Lucy* C)
Now, Lucy. (*She takes Lucy's hand*)

(*They go to Harold, and* LUCY *takes Harold's hand*)

Now let's all run and see how quickly we can go.

(*They scamper off* R)

HAROLD (*as they go*) Why do washerwomans—— (*But we hear
no more*)

TOAD (*half waking again*) And tell cook I'll have three eggs this
morning, and be sure to give them each four minutes. . . . (*He
moves and wriggles, and then slowly sits up*) There, she's pulled the
blinds up, and I told her—— Hallo! (*He looks round him in amaze-
ment*) Wherever—— (*He stands up, looks at his clothes, looks round
him again, and draws a deep breath of happiness*) Aha! (*He chuckles*)
Toad again! (*He comes to* C) Escaped from prison! Eluded his
captors! Evaded his pursuers! The subtle and resourceful Toad!
(*He sits down in the sun, and idly removes a few dead leaves from his
person*)

(*A* FOX *comes by from* L, *stops* LC, *and looks him up and down in
a sarcastic sort of way*)

FOX. Hallo, washerwoman! Half a pair of socks and a pillow-
case short this week. Mind it doesn't occur again.

(FOX *goes off up* R, *whistling*)

TOAD. Silly joke! Where's the humour of it? (*He stands up and
spreads himself*) If he had known! If he had only known who it
was! Not a common washerwoman, but the great, the good, the
entirely glorious Toad!

No. 19

(*He walks round and round in a circle, chanting his song*)

> The world has held great heroes,
>   As history-books have showed;
> But never a name to go down to fame
>   Compared with that of Toad.
>
> The animals sat in the Ark and cried,
>   Their tears in torrents flowed;
> Who was it said, "There's land ahead"?
>   Encouraging Mr Toad!
>
> The Queen and her ladies-in-waiting
>   Sat in the window and sewed;
> She cried, "Look, who's that *handsome* man?"
>   They answered, "Mr Toad."

(*In an ecstasy*) Oh, how clever I am! How clever, how very clever—— (*He breaks off suddenly, as voices are heard crying* "Toad! Toad! There he is! This way!") Oh, misery! Oh, despair! (*Terrified, he rushes into the hollow tree, and burrows under the leaves*)

(*The* Usher, *the* Policeman, *the* Gaoler *and the* Judge *come in from* L *to music*)

Policeman (*down* L) This way, your lordship. I heard him singing. All about himself. Just about here it sounded like. (*He begins to look round*)

(*The* Gaoler *is now up* LC *and the* Usher *up* L)

Judge (c) Not that revolting song he sang when I had the pleasure of sentencing him to twenty years in a dungeon?

Policeman (*crossing* R) That's the song, your lordship. Only he had a new verse to it. Three verses he sang altogether.

Judge. As conceited as the old ones?

Policeman. Worse.

Judge. Dear, dear. (*To the Usher*) What's the penalty for singing conceited songs about yourself? Can I give him another five years?

Policeman. We've got to catch him first.

Usher (*coming down* L) Two years a verse is the usual.

(*The* Gaoler *crosses round to down* R)

Judge. Good. Then that's six years. And say ten for having had the ingratitude to escape from a perfectly clean—(*to the Gaoler*) ventilated, you said?

Gaoler. Well-ventilated.

Judge. Well-ventilated prison. That's another sixteen years. Excellent!

Policeman. We've got to catch him first. But he's about here somewhere, that I do say.

(*All look off* R, *then off* L, *then up stage, then to front*)

Gaoler. Just look in that hollow tree.

Judge. He wouldn't be there, would he? Such a silly place to hide in.

Policeman. Well, you never know. (*He goes to it*)

(Toad, *quaking in his fear, displaces the leaves*)

There's *something* there.

Judge. Something undoubtedly.

(*They all gather round*)

Usher. A bird of some sort, most like. (*He comes* c)

Toad (*brilliantly*) Chirp! Chirp! Chirp!

Policeman. Yes, you're right. Only a bird.

JUDGE. Only a bird. What a pity.

USHER. I knew it was only a bird. We're wasting time here.

JUDGE. True. Lead on, Gaoler.

POLICEMAN. Well, he's not far off.

GAOLER. This way.

(*They all go off* R.
The leaves move again, and then TOAD's *head peeps cautiously out*)

TOAD (*panting with fear*) Oh my! What an ass I am! What a conceited and heedless ass! (*He rises and comes out of the tree*) Swaggering again! Shouting and singing songs again! Sitting about and gassing again! Oh my! (*He looks round cautiously, then explores the clearing. The pursuit has died away*) Ah! That was good! Just a little resource, a little cleverness! "Only a bird." Ha, ha, ha! (*He is standing with his back to the tow-path*)

(*A* HORSE, *dragging a tow-rope, comes along the path from* R, *stops, and puts his head ingratiatingly over Toad's shoulder.* TOAD's *jaw drops. His knees tremble*)

(*Terrified*) All right! I'll come quietly. (*He looks nervously round, sees the horse, and gives a sob of relief*) You quite startled me! I thought it was—— I said I'd come quietly, just to put him off his guard. That was all. Just to—— Hallo! (*He sees the rope*) A barge. Aha!

(*The barge comes on from up* R)

I will hail the owner and pitch him a yarn, and he will give me a lift by a route which is not troubled by fat policemen. Perhaps (*he heaves a sigh*) I may even get some breakfast! (*He crosses* R)

(*The* HORSE *has stopped and is cropping the grass. Evidently he is meant to stop here, for a comfortable-looking* BARGE-WOMAN *comes in, carrying a bag of corn*)

BARGE-WOMAN (*coming down the bank to the horse* C) A nice morning, ma'am.

TOAD (RC) The same to you, ma'am.

BARGE-WOMAN (*holding up the bag*) Give the horse a bit of breakfast. (*She ties the nose-bag on the horse's head*)

(*The* HORSE *turns up stage, hind-quarters to front*)

TOAD (*with meaning*) The horse?

BARGE-WOMAN. Had mine.

TOAD. And a good hearty breakfast I'm sure it was, ma'am.

BARGE-WOMAN. Well, I don't deny I like my vittals. (*She gets a rope from the barge and ties it to the horse's tail*)

TOAD. You're right, ma'am, you're right. (*Casually*) And finished it all up, I daresay—fried ham and eggs and—all of it.

BARGE-WOMAN (*with a laugh*) Pretty well, ma'am, pretty well.

Toad. Ah! (*He is gloomily silent*)

Barge-woman (*having finished with the horse*) You seem in trouble, ma'am.

Toad. Trouble! Here's my married daughter she sends off to me to come at once. So off I comes, not knowing what may be happening. And I've left my business to look after itself—I'm in the washing and laundering line, as you can see, ma'am.

Barge-woman (l *of the horse*) Dear, dear! Where might your married daughter be living?

Toad. Toad Hall, ma'am. (*He crosses to* R *of the horse*) The finest house in these parts for miles around, as no doubt you've heard tell. That is, she lives just close to it. (*He leans over the horse*)

Barge-woman (*also leaning over the horse*) Toad Hall? Why, I'm going that way myself. You come along in the barge with me, and I'll give you a lift.

Toad. I'm sure you're very kind, ma'am.

Barge-woman. Don't mention it. So you're in the washing business. And a fine business you've got too, I daresay, if I'm not making too free in saying so.

Toad. Finest business in the whole country! All the gentry come to me!

Barge-woman. But surely you don't *do* it all yourself, ma'am?

Toad. Oh, I have girls, twenty or thirty of them always at work. But you know what girls are, ma'am. Idle trollops, that's what I call them.

Barge-woman. They are that. And are you very fond of washing?

Toad. I love it. I simply dote on it. Never so happy as when I've got both arms in the wash-tub.

Barge-woman. What a bit of luck meeting you!

Toad (*nervously*) Why, what do you mean?

Barge-woman. Well, look at *me*. I like washing too, same as you. But there's my husband, he has gone off somewhere with the dog. Meantime, how am I to get on with my washing?

Toad. Oh, never mind about the washing.

Barge-woman. It's no good, I keep thinking of that washing. And if it's a pleasure to you to do it, being that fond of it, why then——

Toad (*hastily*) No, no, I mustn't deprive you, not after you've been looking forward to it for weeks, as I expect you have. I'll steer, and then *you* can get on with your washing in your own way.

Barge-woman (*with suspicion*) I don't believe you're a washer-woman at all. (*She gives the* Horse *a hard smack and it starts up stage to the tree*)

Toad (*indignantly*) Of course I'm a washerwoman! Should I be likely to say I was a washerwoman, if I wasn't? It isn't a thing you want to go about saying, if you aren't. Why should I be wearing a washerwoman's clothes if I'm not a washerwoman?

BARGE-WOMAN (*firmly*) Well, if you ask me, ma'am, I should say it's all a piece of deceit. (*She goes to untie the bag from the horse's head*)

TOAD (*with dignity*) Oh, indeed, ma'am!

BARGE-WOMAN. And I say this, ma'am, that if you have a daughter, which I daresay you haven't, I'm sorry for her, having a mother which practises deceit. (*She comes away with the bag, goes to the barge and disappears up* R) And I'll wish you good-morning, ma'am.

(*The* HORSE *moves down stage* LC)

No. 19a

TOAD (*following her up and shouting after her*) You common, low, fat barge-woman, don't you dare to talk to your betters like that. Washerwoman, indeed! I would have you know that I am the Toad, the Terror of the Countryside, the Scourge of Barge-women! Keep your stupid little barge! I prefer—riding! (*He jumps on the horse's back and gallops off* L) The Toad! The Toad!

BARGE-WOMAN (*entering from up* R *and coming to down* R) Help! Help! The notorious Toad! Help!

(*The* POLICEMAN *and the others join in the pursuit. They come on from down* R, *and catch hold of the rope, which is affixed to the horse's tail. But the tail comes out, and they are left with it on the end of the rope*)

ALL. The Toad! The Toad!

CURTAIN

ACT IV

Scene i

No. 20

Scene—*Rat's Riverside Residence.*
In construction it is something like the cabin of a ship. Through the large port-holes at the back, the opposite bank of the river can be seen. (See Photograph of Scene)

Rat *is seated on a keg,* R *of the table* RC, *singing. He is busily cleaning a large heap of pistols, swords and cudgels.*
At a port-hole L *the head of the* Toad, *still wearing his washer-woman's bonnet over one eye, appears suddenly.*

Toad (*from outside*) Help! Help!

Rat (*thoughtfully listening*) Funny! That sounded like Toad's voice.

Toad. Help!

Rat. Yes, if Toad had been anywhere but where he is, poor unfortunate animal, I should have said——

Toad. Help! Help!

Rat (*turning round*) It is! (*He rises and crosses in front of the table to Toad*) Toady! However——

Toad. Give us a hand, Rat. I'm about done.

(Toad *kicks,* Rat *pulls, and he tumbles in on to the floor*)

Rat. There!

Toad (*gasping*) Oh! . . . Oh! . . . Oh!

Rat (*helping him up*) Come on the sofa a bit, won't you?

(*They move to the sofa* LC)

Toad (*faintly*) Thank you, dear Ratty, thank you. (*He flops on to the sofa*)

(Rat *goes to the cupboard up* C, *for a bottle of ginger-beer*)

Rat. Here, drink this. You're about done. (*He hands Toad the bottle*)

Toad (*drinking*) Ah! (*He drinks again*) That's better. I shall soon be all right.

Rat (*looking at him*) Poor old Toady! (*He puts the bottle back in the cupboard, then comes back to Toad*) And wet as wet. . . . And am I wrong, or *are* you disguised in parts as a washerwoman who has seen better days?

Toad (*complacently*) Aha!

Rat. That's more like you. Escaped, eh? In disguise?

53

TOAD (*more complacently*) Aha! (*He begins to sit up and take notice*)

RAT. That's much better. We'll soon have you all right.

TOAD. It takes a good deal to put me out, Ratty. Just a passing faintness which might happen to any one who had been through what *I've* been through.

RAT (*crossing to* L *of the table*) You've been through a lot, I expect.

TOAD. My dear Ratty, the times I've been through since I saw you last, you simply can't think!

RAT. Yes. Well, when you've got those horrible things off, and cleaned yourself up a bit——

TOAD. The times! Such trials, such sufferings, and all so nobly borne!

RAT. You'll find some dry clothes in there. (*He points towards the door* L)

TOAD. Such escapes, such disguises, such subterfuges, and all so cleverly planned and carried out!

RAT. Quite so. Well——

TOAD. Been in prison—(*rising*) got out of it, of course! Stole a horse—rode away on it. Humbugged everybody—made 'em do exactly as I wanted. Oh, I *am* a smart Toad, and no mistake. (*He goes up to* L *of the cupboard and leans on it*) Now what do you think my very last exploit was?

RAT (*severely*) I don't know, Toad. But seeing where it was I found you, and the state you were in, I should say that somebody had dropped you into the river, and then thrown mud at you. It isn't a thing to boast about, really it isn't, Toad.

TOAD. Pooh, that was nothing. (*He crosses to down* R) I just happened to be—to be heading a pursuit—on my horse—right in front of everybody else, in my usual way—(*he crosses to* LC) and accidentally, not noticing the river in the enthusiasm of the chase —and the horse stopping a moment or two before I did——

RAT (*warningly*) Toad!

TOAD (*going up to* L *of the cupboard*) But I wasn't going to tell you about that. Now what do you think——

RAT (*taking him by the shoulders*) Toad!

TOAD. Here, hold on a moment. I just want to tell you——

RAT. Toad, you will go at once, and see if you can possibly make yourself look like a respectable animal again, for a more shabby, bedraggled, disreputable-looking object than you are now, I never set eyes on.

TOAD (*with dignity*) You can hardly realize, Ratty, to whom you are——

RAT. Now stop swaggering and arguing and be off. Badger and Mole will be in directly——

TOAD (*airily*) Oh, ah! Yes, of course, the Mole and the Badger. What's become of them, the dear fellows? I had forgotten all about them.

Rat (*gravely*) Well may you ask!

Toad. Why, what——

Rat. You will hear in good time. Badger himself may prefer to break the news to you. Be off now, and prepare yourself—why, what's the matter?

Toad (*who has wandered in front of a mirror on the flat up* L, *and is regarding himself with horror*) Is this glass of yours all right?

Rat. Of course. Why?

Toad. I hoped—— You see, it's the first time I—— You're quite right, Ratty. Nobody could carry off a costume like this. (*Meekly*) I'll go and change.

(Toad *goes out* L.

Rat, *left alone, fetches duster, pan and brush, and begins to clean up after Toad, murmuring,* "Dear, dear!" *to himself, and* "Well, I never!"

While he is so engaged Badger *and* Mole *come in* R. Badger *crosses in front of the table to above the sofa* LC. Mole *goes to the keg* R *of the table*)

Rat (*eagerly*) Hallo, here you are! I say, what do you think?

Mole (*sitting on the keg*) Too tired to think, Ratty, and that's a fact.

Rat. Yes, but——

Badger (*gruffly*) Nobody thinks nowadays. (*He lies on the sofa*) That's the trouble. Too much action, not enough thought.

Rat. Yes, but——

Mole (*to Rat*) He's a bit low, just now. We've had a hard day. He'll be all right directly.

Rat (L *of the table*) Yes, but what do you think? Toad's back.

Mole (*jumping up*) Toad! Back where?

Rat. Here!

Mole. Where?

Rat (*with a jerk of the head*) Cleaning. You ought to have seen him, Mole. He'd have made you laugh.

Badger (*with his eyes shut*) Unhappy animal!

Mole. Escaped?

Rat (*nodding*) 'M. Came in five minutes ago. In such a state.

Badger. I would speak with him.

Rat. He's just having a wash.

Badger (*severely*) This is no time for washing. (*He sits up on the sofa*) We have work before us tonight. Hard fighting. Washing can wait. Where do you think *I* should have been if, at the crisis of my life, I had stopped to wash? Where would my revered father have been, if he had put soap before strategy? Where would my beloved grandfather——

Mole (*loudly, rising*) Toady!

Toad (*from outside*) Hallo, Mole, old fellow!

Badger. Thank you, Mole. (*He closes his eyes again*)

MOLE (*to Rat*) I heard all about his beloved grandfather this morning. Most interesting.

(TOAD *comes in from* L. *He is almost his old self*)

TOAD (*cheerily*) Hallo, you fellows!
MOLE (*delightedly*) Toady!

(TOAD *goes to below the table*)

BADGER (*solemnly rising*) Welcome home, Toad! Alas! what am I saying? Home, indeed. This is a poor home-coming. Unhappy Toad! (*He sinks on to the sofa again*)
MOLE. Fancy having *you* back! And today of all days! To think that you have escaped from prison, you clever, intelligent Toad.
TOAD. Clever? Oh, no! I'm not clever, really. Badger doesn't think so. Rat doesn't think so. I've only broken out of the strongest prison in England, that's all. And disguised myself, and gone about the country on my horse humbugging everybody, that's all. Clever? Oh dear, no. (*He goes up to the* R *port-hole at back*)
RAT. Oh, Toady!
TOAD (*turning and coming down to above the table*) Well, I shall be strolling along to Toad Hall. One does get appreciated at home. Mole, if you like to drop in to coffee one evening, and care to hear a few of my milder adventures——
MOLE (*sadly*) Oh, Toady, and you haven't heard!
TOAD. Heard what? Quick, don't spare me! What haven't I heard?
MOLE. The Stoats and the Weasels!
RAT (L *of the table*) The Wild-Wooders!
MOLE. And how they've been and gone——
RAT. And taken Toad Hall——
MOLE. And been living there ever since——
RAT. Going on simply anyhow——
MOLE. Lying in bed half the day——
RAT. Breakfast at all hours——
MOLE. Eating your grub and drinking your drink——
RAT. And making bad jokes about you, and singing vulgar songs——
MOLE. About—— (*He hesitates*)
RAT. About—— (*He hesitates*)
MOLE. Well, about prisons and magistrates and policemen.
RAT. Horrid personal songs with no humour in them.
MOLE. That's what's happened, Toad. And it's no good pretending it hasn't.
RAT. And they're all telling everybody that they've come to Toad Hall to stay for good.
TOAD. Oh, have they! I'll jolly soon see about that!
RAT. Yes, but how?
TOAD (*doubtfully*) Well—well—well, what I shall do——

RAT. Of course, what you *ought* to do——

MOLE. No, he oughtn't. Nothing of the sort. What he ought to do is, he ought to——

TOAD. Well, I shan't do it anyhow. I've been ordered about quite enough. It's my house we're talking about, and I know exactly what to do, and I'll tell you. I'm going to——

BADGER (*rising from the sofa and standing* R *of it*) Be quiet, all of you!

(*They are silent*)

Toad!

TOAD (*meekly, coming down to Badger*) Yes, Badger?

BADGER. When you got into trouble a short time ago, and brought disgrace upon your own name, and shame and sorrow upon your friends, I resolved that on your return from your enforced seclusion, I would take the first opportunity of pointing out to you the folly of your ways.

TOAD (*meekly*) Yes, Badger. Thank you, Badger.

BADGER. I even went so far as to jot down a few rough notes on the subject. (*He points to the sofa*)

(TOAD *takes the hint and sits at the* R *end of it*)

Where are they, Rat?

RAT (*getting paper from the top shelf of the cupboard, and handing it to Badger*) Here you are.

BADGER. Thank you. (*Reading*) "To make suet dumplings——"

RAT. It's on the other side.

BADGER. Ah yes, here we are.

TOAD (*meekly*) I'd rather have the bit about the dumplings, if it's all the same to you.

BADGER (*reading*) "(1) Conceit and its consequence. (2) Reverend Uncle, grief of. (3) Toad, whither tending?" But the moment for all this is past.

TOAD (*humbly*) Just as you like, Badger, old man.

BADGER. The moment is past, because it is obvious now to everybody here where your folly has brought you. Toad Hall is in the hands of your enemies. Sentries guard it day and night. Unhappy Toad.

TOAD (*bursting into tears*) Alas, alas! Toad Hall, that desirable riverside residence, in the hands of Stoats and Weasels! This is, indeed, the end of everything! (*He rolls on to the sofa in his grief*)

BADGER. Not quite the end. Now I'm going to tell you a great secret which I heard from your father. There is an underground passage that leads from the River Bank right up into the middle of Toad Hall.

(BADGER *joins Toad on the sofa.* RAT *comes down to* R *of the sofa.* MOLE *to* R *of Rat*)

Tonight the Chief Weasel is giving a banquet. It's his birthday. While they are all feasting, careless of the morrow, we four, armed to the teeth, will creep silently, by way of the passage, into the butler's pantry.

TOAD. Ah! that squeaky board in the butler's pantry!

BADGER. Armed to the teeth, you and Rat, by one door——

RAT (*looking up*) Yes, Badger.

BADGER. And me and Mole by the other——

MOLE. Yes, Badger.

BADGER. Also armed to the teeth—we shall——

MOLE. Creep out of the pantry—— (*He runs up to the table excitedly, and gets a pistol*)

RAT. With our pistols, and swords and sticks—— (*He goes up to the cupboard and gets a cutlass*)

BADGER. And rush in on them——

TOAD (*rising and crossing to* RC—*ecstatically*) And whack 'em and whack 'em and whack 'em.

BADGER (*rising*) Exactly. (*He crosses over and pats Toad on the back*) You have caught the spirit of it perfectly. Good Toad!

TOAD. I'll learn 'em to steal my house.

RAT (*L of the table*) Teach 'em, Toad, not learn 'em.

BADGER. But we don't *want* to teach 'em. Toad's quite right. We want to *learn* 'em, and, what's more, we're going to.

No. 20a

(*Quartet:* TOAD, BADGER, RAT *and* MOLE)

ALL.   When night comes on and the Owls are hooting,
And Rabbits back to their holes are scooting,
And Weasel's wearing his ev'ning suiting.
A-wallopping we will go.
A-wallopping we will go.
A-wallopping we will go.
We'll take off our braces and take off our coats
And *learn* the Weasels and Ferrets and Stoats.

BADGER. Who says so?

RAT. Rat says so.

MOLE. Mole says so.

TOAD. Toad says so.

BADGER. Badger says so.

ALL.   We'll take off our braces and take off our coats
And *talk* to Weasels and Ferrets and Stoats.

MOLE. I haven't got any braces.

RAT. Mole hasn't got any braces.

BADGER. Toad will lend him a pair of

TOAD. Embroider'd silk

BADGER. Braces.

MOLE. Ah!

ALL.   We'll take off our braces and take off our coats
          And *wallop* the Weasels and Ferrets and Stoats,
          We'll take off our braces and take off our coats
          And *wallop* the Weasels and Ferrets and Stoats,
          And *wallop* the Weasels and Ferrets and Stoats,
          When night comes on and the Bats are batting,
          And Rabbits back in their holes are chatting,
          And Weasel's wearing his opera hatting,
          A-wallopping we will go.
          A-wallopping we will go.
          A-wallopping we will go.
          We'll take off our collars and take off our coats
          And *learn* the Weasels and Ferrets and Stoats.
BADGER.   Who says so?
RAT.   Rat says so.
MOLE.   Mole says so.
TOAD.   Toad says so.
BADGER.   *Badger says so.*
ALL.   We'll take off our collars and take off our coats
          And talk to Weasels and Ferrets and Stoats.
MOLE.   I haven't got any collar.
TOAD.   Mole hasn't got any collar.
BADGER.   Rat will lend him a nice clean,
RAT.   Fairly clean collar.
MOLE.   Ah!
ALL.   We'll take off our braces and collars and coats
          And *wallop* the Weasels and Ferrets and Stoats,
          We'll take off our braces and collars and coats
          And *wallop* the Weasels and Ferrets and Stoats,
          And *wallop* the Weasels and Ferrets and Stoats.
TOAD, RAT *and* MOLE. Badger, Badger, Badger, Badger says so.
BADGER. I say so.

Now then, to rest, all of you. We start at nine o'clock, and we
must be fresh for it. (*He settles down on the sofa*)
RAT. I'll just get the lanterns trimmed.

     (RAT *goes out* L)

MOLE (*going to* R *of the cupboard for sacking, bringing it to* L *of the
table, and lying down on it*) Badger's right. I want a rest.
TOAD (*sitting on the keg* R *of the table*) Yes, we must rest.

No. 20b

(TOAD *begins to chuckle.* MOLE, *eyes closed, takes no notice.* TOAD
glances at him and chuckles more loudly. MOLE *lazily opens an eye*)

MOLE (*sleepily*) Eh?
TOAD (*laughing heartily*) I was just thinking—most amusing

thing—really rather funny—I was in a hollow tree—and a policeman—well, a whole army of 'em, was looking for me—and one of
'em said, "Is that a bird?"—ha, ha, ha!—really, very funny—"Is
that a bird or what?"—and what do you think *I* did?—ha, ha, ha!
—I said—— (*and so on*)

(MOLE *sleeps*)

Black Out

CURTAIN

SCENE 2

No. 21

SCENE—*The Secret Passage. (See Photograph of Scene)*

The four conspirators steal in up L—BADGER, RAT, MOLE, TOAD.
BADGER *and* MOLE *carry the lanterns. They are all armed to the teeth.*

BADGER (*to Rat*) H'sh!
RAT (*to Mole*) H'sh!
MOLE (*to Toad*) H'sh!
TOAD (*loudly*) What?
THE OTHERS. H'sh!
TOAD. Oh, all right.

(*Positions from* L *to* R *are:* TOAD, MOLE, RAT, BADGER)

BADGER. We are now in the secret passage, but not yet under
the house. For the moment silence is not absolutely necessary, but
later on——
TOAD (*airily*) Quite so, quite so!
BADGER. Now, it's all understood? Mole and I burst into the
banqueting hall by the east door, and drive them towards the
west door, where Rat and Toad——
TOAD (*impatiently*) That's all right, Badger. Let's get at 'em.
BADGER. Rat, you're responsible for the operations on the
western front. You understand? . . . What's the matter?
RAT (*who is trying to read something by the light of Mole's lantern*)
Just before we start, hadn't we better make sure we've got everything? (*Reading*) One belt, one sword, one cutlass, one cudgel,
one pair pistols, one policeman's truncheon, one policeman's
whistle——

(TOAD *blows his loudly*)

BADGER (*alarmed*) What's that?
MOLE (*reproachfully*) Toad!
BADGER (*sternly*) Was that you, Toad?
TOAD (*meekly*) I just wanted to be sure it worked.

BADGER. Now, Toad, I warn you solemnly, if I have any trouble from *you*, you'll be sent back, as sure as fate.

TOAD (*humbly*) Oh, Badger!

BADGER. Well, I warn you.

RAT. One policeman's whistle, two pairs of handcuffs, bandages, sticking-plaster, flask, sandwich-case. Now, has everybody got that?

BADGER (*with a laugh*) I've got it, but I'm going to do all I want to do with this here stick.

RAT. It's just as you like, Badger. It's only that I don't want you to blame me afterwards and say that I'd forgotten anything.

BADGER. Well, well! But no pistols, unless we have to. We shall only be shooting each other.

RAT. Pistols in reserve, of course. Eh, Moly?

MOLE. Of course. Eh, Toad?

TOAD (*who is examining his*) Of course.

(*It goes off with a tremendous bang. Everybody jumps*)

MOLE (*reproachfully*) Toad!

BADGER. Toad? You don't mean to say that that was Toad again? After what I've just said?

TOAD. I—I just—I didn't——

BADGER. Very well then, you go back.

TOAD (*falling on his knees*) Oh, please, Badger, please!

BADGER. No! I can't take the risk.

TOAD. Oh, Badger, please. After all I've been through—and my own house too. You *mustn't* send me back.

BADGER (*wavering*) I ought to.

MOLE. Look here, I'll go last and keep an eye on him——

(TOAD *and* MOLE *change places*)

RAT. And we'll take his pistols and his whistle away. (*He does so*)

BADGER. Well——

RAT. We'll leave 'em here, see. (*He puts them on the ground by the entrance up* L) Just here. It might be very useful, if we had to beat a retreat, to find a couple of freshly primed pistols and a policeman's whistle to fall back on. That'll be all right, Badger.

BADGER (*gruffly*) Very well. (*He leads on*) Now then, no more talking. From this moment absolute silence.

TOAD (*very humbly*) Just before we begin the silence, Badger——

BADGER (*after waiting in silence*) Well, what is it?

TOAD. A-a-a-a—tishoo!

(*Mole's lantern goes out*)

MOLE. Oh, he's blown my lantern out!

TOAD. That's all. I felt it coming. Now I won't say another word.

No. 21a

(*All creep stealthily towards the entrance up* R, *then run back* L *on low note in music. They go* R *again:* MOLE *turns* L, *and all jump on low note in music. Eventually* BADGER *exits* R, *followed by* RAT *and* TOAD. MOLE, *who is by this time down* L, *turns round to find that he is alone, and hastily exits up* R *after the others*)

Black Out

CURTAIN

SCENE 3

No. 22

SCENE—*The Banqueting-room—a magnificent apartment—in Toad Hall.* (*See Photograph of Scene*)

It being the CHIEF WEASEL's *birthday, a banquet is in progress. The hero of the occasion, a laurel wreath on his brow, sits above the main table, his admirers, Stoats, Ferrets, etc., around him. There is a ballet of Weasels, Stoats and Ferrets, and then all return to the table. Pressed for a few words, the* CHIEF WEASEL *rises. All sit in a semicircle on the floor, below the table, and facing up stage.*

CHIEF WEASEL. Friends and Fellow Animals. Before we part this evening I have one final toast to propose. (*Hear, hear!*) It is a toast which on all occasions has something of solemnity in it, something even of sadness, but never more so than on this occasion. "Absent Friends." (*Hear, hear!*) Absent Friends. With this toast I couple first the name of our kind host, Mr Toad. (*Loud laughter*) Although unable to be present himself tonight— (*laughter*) owing to a previous engagement—(*laughter*) Mr Toad has generously put his entire establishment at our disposal for as long as we like to make use of it. (*Loud laughter*) We all know Toad —(*Hear, hear!* (good Toad, wise Toad, modest Toad. (*Laughter*) It is a personal sorrow to every one of us that he is not amongst us tonight. Let me sing you a little song which I have composed on this subject. (*Hear, hear!*)

No. 23

(*The* CHIEF WEASEL *comes round to below the table into the circle*)

Toad he went a-pleasuring
    Gaily down the road—
They put him in prison for twenty years:
    Poor—old—Toad!

Toad he had a beautiful house,
A most refined abode—
They put him in prison for twenty years:
Poor—old—Toad!

Toad he had much money and goods
All carefully bestowed—
They put him in prison for twenty years:
Poor—old—Toad!

Chief Weasel. Chorus, please.

Poor—old—Toad!
Poor—old—Toad!
They put him in prison for twenty years:
Poor—old—Toad!

(*Loud applause.* Chief Weasel *goes above the table again. All rise and move up to front of the table*)

Chief Weasel. Fellow animals, I give you the toast—"Absent Friends!" (*He drinks*)
All (*drinking*) Absent Friends!
A Deep Voice Outside. Absent Friends!
All (*to each other*) What's that? . . . What is it? . . . I didn't hear anything . . . Nonsense . . .

(*The door opens.* Badger *and* Mole *rush in up stage* RC. Badger *goes to* R *of the table,* Mole *to above the table*)

Badger (*his war-cry*) Up the Badger!
Mole (*his*) A Mole! A Mole!
Badger (*wielding his cudgel*) Lay on to 'em, boys.

(Badger *biffs the* Chief Ferret, *who goes under the table. He then turns his attention to the group* RC, *and biffs them off* R *and off down* R)

Mole (*between blows, doing his bit* L *of the stage*) Sorry we're late, Weasel—(*biff!*)—but many thanks all the same—(*biff!*)—for the kind invitation. (*Biff!*)

No. 24

Chief Weasel. The other door! Quick!

(*The* Chief Weasel, Stoat *and* Ferret *rush to the door down* L, *but as they reach the door it opens and* Toad *and* Rat *charge in*)

Toad (*terribly*) I've come home, Weasel. (*He makes for him*) How are *you*? (*Bang!*) Toad he went a-pleasuring, did he! (*Bang!*) I'll pleasure you! (*Bang!*)
The Enemy (*variously*) Help! . . . Mercy! . . . All *right*, **all right!** . . . I say, *shut* up!

BADGER. Wallop 'em, boys. Keep walloping!

(*Some of the enemy are showing fight, some are escaping through the doors and windows, some are begging for mercy with uplifted paws*)

RAT (*to one of the weaker brethren*) Surrender, do you? All right. Get in that corner there.

(*There is a small rush for "that corner there" down* L)

MOLE (*seeking whom he can devour*) A Mole! A Mole! (*To an unhappy Stoat*) Hallo, were *you* looking for anything? (*Biff!*) Just wanted to say good-bye? (*Biff!*) *Good*-bye! (*Biff!*) Sorry you can't stop. (*He biffs him out up* L)

TOAD (*to a terrified Stoat*) Good evening! (*Bringing him down* C) Do you sing at all?

STOAT. N-no, sir, please, sir.

TOAD. Not just a *little* song?

STOAT. N-no, sir. I—I never l-learnt singing.

TOAD (*swinging his club*) Not just a *funny* little song about a poor old Toad?

STOAT (*with an effort*) N-no, sir.

TOAD (*ingratiatingly*) Try!

STOAT (*foolishly—in a high squeaky voice*) Poor—old—Toad!

TOAD (*furiously*) I'll learn you to sing!

(*With a squeal the* STOAT *scurries into Rat's corner down* L)

RAT (*getting in front of Toad*) All prisoners here, Toad. I'm looking after them. (*He walks up and down in front of them, pistol in hand*)

(TOAD *and* BADGER *biff the remainder off* R.

    As BADGER *re-enters down* R, MOLE, *who has come down from up* L, *mistakes him, in his excitement for an adversary. They fight, discover their mistake, and shake hands*)

BADGER. There! That's the lot! (*He wipes his brow*) A pity! I was just beginning to enjoy it. (*Crossing down* L *to Rat*) What about your little party, Rat?

RAT. They've surrendered. I thought they might come in useful, waiting on us and so on.

BADGER. If any of 'em *wants* to go on for a bit longer——

CHORUS. No, sir, please, sir.

BADGER. Ah! (*He looks round the room*)

(TOAD *has entered from down* R *and is conducting an imaginary battle with a particularly stubborn adversary*)

TOAD (*getting his blow in*) Aha! (*Dodging an imaginary one*) That's no good. (*Getting another in*) More like *that!* . . .

BADGER (*crossing to Toad* RC *and biffing him over the head*) Hallo!

(TOAD, *recalled to himself, breaks off the engagement rather sheepishly*)

Now then, Toad, stir your stumps, and look lively. I want some grub, I do. We've got your house back for you, and you don't offer us so much as a sandwich.

RAT. Just a moment, Badger. What about the sentries?

BADGER. Sentries, yes.

RAT. They may be still at their posts.

TOAD. Sentries, pooh! They've run away far enough by now, haven't they, Mole?

MOLE. If they're wise they have. (*He moves up to L of the table*)

RAT. I think it would be safer if Mole and I just——

BADGER (*crossing to Rat*) Sensible Rat. There spoke the voice of wisdom. (*Picking up his cudgel*) You and I and Mole——

RAT. Don't you bother, Badger. Mole and I——

BADGER (*grimly, moving to LC*) When I go walloping I *go* walloping.

TOAD (*going to R of Badger*) So do I. Come on, I'll lead the way.

BADGER. You will do nothing of the sort, Toad. You've asked us to stay to supper and we're staying to supper. Well, where is the supper? If this isn't your house, say so, and Mole can entertain us.

(BADGER *exits up* L)

RAT (*indicating the prisoners*) They'll help you get it ready, Toady.

(RAT *goes off after Badger*)

TOAD (*reluctantly*) Oh, all right.

MOLE (*to Toad*) Don't forget the wine, Toad. We shall want to drink your health, and you'll have to make a speech.

TOAD (*cheering up*) Oh, right, right. That's all right, leave that to me.

(MOLE *goes out up* L. TOAD *is left with the now penitent prisoners —about eight of the smaller Stoats and Ferrets*)

(*To his slaves*) Now then, bustle up!

(*They bustle up eagerly*)

CHORUS. Yes, sir, coming, sir!

TOAD. Get busy.

CHORUS. Yes, sir, please, sir!

TOAD. I owe you a leathering apiece, as it is.

CHORUS. Please, sir, no, sir!

TOAD. Well, get busy, and perhaps I won't say any more about it.

(*They are very busy and the hall begins to look tidy again. When they have finished picking up the debris, they come down* LC *and arrange*

themselves in line diagonally across the stage from down L *to up* C,
below the table)

(*Down* C) Got a pencil, any of you?

ONE OF THEM. Yes, sir. (*He gives Toad a pencil*)

TOAD (*taking it*) Thanks. . . . All right, don't hang about, get
busy. (*He takes a piece of paper from his pocket and begins to write*)

THE PRISONERS (*whispering to each other*) He's writing . . . He's
writing a letter . . . It isn't a letter . . . It's *my* pencil he's using
. . . I wonder who he's writing to . . . Shall we ask him what he's
writing? . . . I will if you will . . . *You* ask him, it's your pencil
. . . No, you . . . all right, I don't mind . . . Well, go on then.

THE BRAVE ONE. Please, sir——

TOAD (*proudly*) There!

THE BRAVE ONE. Please, sir——

TOAD. Now, I daresay all you young fellows are wondering
what I've been doing?

CHORUS. Please, sir, yes, sir.

TOAD. Well, I've just been jotting down a few rough notes.

CHORUS. Oo, sir.

TOAD. Just a few notes for a little entertainment I have
sketched out—a little informal singsong or conversazione to cele-
brate my return.

CHORUS. Yes, sir, thank you, sir.

TOAD. Something like this—

(1) Speech—By Toad.

And then I make a note. "There will be other speeches by Toad
during the evening." Just so as to reassure people.

CHORUS. Yes, sir.

TOAD. (2) Address—By Toad.

Synopsis—you all know what that means, of course?

CHORUS. Please, sir, no, sir. Sorry, sir.

TOAD. Well, it just means—well, you'll see what it means
directly. It's just a sort of synopsis.

CHORUS. Yes, sir.

TOAD. (3) Imitations of Various Bird Notes. By Toad.

(4) Song—By Toad. (Composed by Himself.)

(5) Other compositions by Toad. (Sung by the Composer.)

(6) Song. "For He's a Jolly Good Fellow." (Sung by Badger,
Rat, and Mole.)

CHORUS. Oo, sir.

TOAD. That's all, just a few rough notes. Of course it may
shape a little differently as the evening goes on. There are one or
two conjuring tricks which I used to know—something to do with
three billiard balls and a globe of goldfish—they may come back
to me or they may not. We shall see.

CHORUS. Yes, sir, thank you, sir.

THE BRAVE ONE. Could you give us the song now, sir?

TOAD (*pleased*) Give it you now, eh?
CHORUS. Oo, please, sir.
TOAD. Well, well. (*He gets up and walks to the middle of the room*)
THE BRAVE ONE (*picking up the Chief Weasel's wreath which is on the table*) Wouldn't you like to wear this, sir?
TOAD. You think—eh?—— Well, perhaps you're right. (*He puts it on*)
CHORUS. Oo, *sir!*
TOAD. Suits me, eh?
CHORUS. Please, sir, yes, sir.
TOAD. Some people can wear 'em and some can't. You have the manner or you haven't. There it is. You can't explain it.
CHORUS. Yes, sir. Where will you stand, sir?
THE BRAVE ONE (*bringing a chair from the table*) Won't you stand on this, sir?
TOAD (*modestly mounting*) Well, perhaps——
CHORUS. Oo, *sir!*
TOAD. Now this is just a *little* song, and it's called "When the Toad came Home".
CHORUS. Yes, sir.
TOAD. There's only one verse at present, but it can be sung any number of times.
THE BRAVE ONE. Yes, sir. May we all sing it?
TOAD. Certainly, certainly. It is really composed with the idea of being sung by a great many people.

No. 25

CHORUS. Yes, sir. (*They group themselves round him, expectantly*)
TOAD (*solemnly*) "When the Toad came Home."
(*Singing*) The Toad—came home!
There was panic in the parlour, there was howling in the hall,
There was crying in the cow-shed and a snorting in the stall,
There was smashing in of window, there was crashing in of door,
There was bashing of the enemy who fainted on the floor,
      When the Toad—came home!

(*All the prisoners dance in a circle round Toad, singing this song.* TOAD *stands wreathed above them, raptly enjoying it.*

In the middle of the second verse BADGER, RAT *and* MOLE *enter up* L *and come to down* L)

BADGER (*appalled*) Toad! Get down at once!

(TOAD *does not hear him. He is far away. The singers finish their verse, but go on dancing round the hero*)

MOLE (*reproachfully*) Toady!
RAT (*to Badger*) It's no good. I know him. He's practically in a trance. Let him have his evening out.
MOLE. We'll talk to him in the morning.

RAT. Talking's no good to Toad. He'll always come back to what he is.

BADGER (*grimly*) All the same, I'll talk to him.

RAT. But let him have his hour first.

BADGER. Oh, all right.

(*They stand watching. The dancers are singing again now . . .*)

MOLE (*apologetically*) You know, there's something about that tune . . . It's only just . . . I shan't be . . . (*And suddenly he is in the circle, dancing and singing*)

(*The chorus is repeated. At the finish* BADGER *speaks*)

BADGER. He's very young still, is Mole.

RAT. Y-yes.

BADGER. The best of fellows, of course. But young, young.

RAT. Y-yes . . . All the same, I don't see why . . . I mean, after all . . . I . . . well, I . . . Excuse me! (*And now he, too, is in the circle*)

(*But others seem to have heard the news. The* JURY *come on from up* RC, *singing and dancing. They join the circle*)

JURY. There were calls from all the neighbours, there were letters from afar—

(*They are followed by the* JUDGE *and the* USHER)

JUDGE. There was groaning on the Bench——

USHER. —and there was moaning at the Bar.

(*Then* PHOEBE——)

PHOEBE. There was tooting on the piccolo and fluting on the pipes.

(*—and the* WASHERWOMAN *and* BARGE-WOMAN)

WOMEN. There was starching of 'is sockses and a washing of 'is wipes,

ALL. When the Toad came home, When the Toad came home.

(*Enter* ALFRED, *dancing*)

ALFRED. There was shrieking in the gear-box, there was trumpeting of horn,

And the elephant was jealous and the parrot felt forlorn.

ALL. There were speeches from the gentry, there was moistening of throats,

(*Enter the* POLICEMAN)

POLICEMAN. And a moistening of pencils and a taking down of notes.

ALL. When the Toad came home, When the Toad came home.

(*Now they are all round Toad, singing and dancing; all but* Badger)

Badger. Well, well, well! (*Doubtfully*) Well—— (*Less doubtfully*) W-w-well? (*His mind made up*) Oh, well! (*He joins the dancers, and hobbles stiffly round with them, followed by* Alfred)

All. There was welcoming to Badger, when he joined the merry throng.

Badger. I can do it for a little but I can't go on for long . . .

(*And so on. The incense of their adoration streams up to the belaurelled* Toad, *and with a long sigh of happiness he closes his eyes.*

Suddenly the lights fade out, and when they come up again we are down by the willows again, on the river bank)

EPILOGUE

THE WIND IN THE WILLOWS

It is Spring again. The wind is whispering in the willows that fringe the river. Faintly we hear its elfin music.

Among her daffodils lies MARIGOLD, *in tumbled sleep. The dead leaves in the hollow rise and fall; they fall apart as an old grey* BADGER *heaves himself into the sunlight. Curiously he sniffs at Marigold, and then lumbers away. A* WATER-RAT *twinkles out of his hole in the bank: a* MOLE *laboriously takes the air; they, too, pass the time of day with Marigold before following in the wake of the Badger. Last of all comes a* TOAD. "Ah, Marigold, Marigold!"—*and so, waddling jauntily, after the others* . . .*

But NURSE *is getting impatient. From afar her voice comes to us off* L.

NURSE (*off* L) Marigold! Marigold! It's time we went, dear!

> Wind in the willows is whispering low,
> Still is the meadow which dreams in the sun,
> Blue overhead and green your bed,
> Sleep, little people, to Lullaby.

(MARIGOLD *sighs gently, and stirs a little in her sleep. At the end of Nurse's song she wakes up and waves farewell to them all*)

CURTAIN

PROPERTY PLOT

PROLOGUE

On stage—Grass mat in front of ground row RC. *On it:* small bunch of bluebells,
    1 doz. daffodils in basket
    Tree log LC
    In front of log: rug, knitting-needles, wool and basket

ACT I
To be set before rise of Curtain on Prologue

On stage—Tree-trunk L and loose leaves
    Luncheon-basket on ground behind door in cut-cloth up LC
    In luncheon-basket: 4 sandwiches, 2 ginger-beer bottles (one with loose
       cork), 2 meringues, 2 lemonade bottles, 1 cold ham, 1 cold chicken,
       4 oranges and 4 bananas, 3 plates, 1 table napkin, 1 strap on basket
    Corkscrew, telescope, padded cudgel for RAT behind door in cut-
       cloth up LC

Off stage—Push motor-horn
    Wooden ratchet crash
    Wood slam
    Thunder sheet (up stage)
    Caravan with horse collar and ropes attached, and with whip on top
    White horse for two men

Hand properties—Goggles ⎫
             Gloves   ⎬for TOAD
             Dandy-cane ⎭
             Walking-stick for BADGER

ACT II
SCENE 1

On stage—Profile bush with apron on two hooks and dummy
    Bell-pull L of bush RC
    In front of bush, a piece of canvas 5 feet wide, 3 feet deep
    On piece of canvas small old doormat about 2 feet wide and small
       rusty old door-scraper
    Loose leaves to cover doormat and door-scraper

Off stage—Owl hoot
    Windwheel
    Hand bell

Hand properties—Lantern alight ⎫
             Two pistols   ⎬for RAT in R corner
             Cudgel   ⎭

SCENE 2
To be set before rise of Curtain on Scene 1

On stage—1 armchair above door R
    Rustic table RC
    Behind table, 1 occasional chair
    L of table, 1 occasional chair
    In front of table, stool
    On table: supper laid for three people: 3 plates, 3 knives, 3 forks,

3 spoons, 1 bottle Military pickles opened, 1 property loaf of bread on board, 1 property joint of beef with fork in it on dish, small paste sandwiches on plate

Poker at fireplace LC

The Times newspaper in armchair R of fireplace

Sit-on shelf for mantelpiece

On mantelpiece: churchwarden pipes in old pewter mug, box of safety matches

Large key on flat between fireplace and window

Small log fire on base (not alight) in front of fireplace

Off stage—Hang-over bell and door-knocker
      Lamp on stick (lamp alight) for Carol Singers

Hand properties—From previous scene: Lantern
               Two pistols for RAT
               Goggles, gloves, cane and hat for TOAD
               Coins for RAT

N.B.—Ready for repeat of Scene after Black Out

Basket to hold things cleared from table *off*

Small camp bed. *On it:* blanket, mattress

Sacking, pillow and 2 sheets

Trick stool with umbrella off L

Potatoes and knife in pot bowl

White apron for RAT between window and door up R

ACT III

SCENE 1

On stage—Stony slab to seat 3 people down R
         3 stone slabs for Judge's throne C
         Hollow tree-trunk up C
         Jury Box: Two slabs of stone and twelve toadstools on stands up and down LC
         1 writing-desk for Judge's throne
         White horse

Hand properties—Large red quill pen ⎫
              Watch and chain   ⎬ for JUDGE
              Large pair of glasses ⎭
              Large pencil
              3 sheets of cartridge-paper with large seal and ribbons for USHER
              Axe for GAOLER and leather apron

N.B.—Ready for change in Scene 2, The Dungeon

Occasional chair, small rustic table

Pile of sacking and stool off in R corner

Bolt and chain effect ⎱
Door slam   ⎰ off L

Menu card

Wooden tray. *On it:* tumbler (wired on) and crust of bread. For PHOEBE off L

Second wooden tray. *On it:* tea-cup and saucer and covered salver with buttered toast. For PHOEBE

Bundle of clothes for WASHERWOMAN

Piece of trick line, 6 feet long, for WASHERWOMAN off L

Coins ready to hand to TOAD as he goes on from R corner

Setting of furniture during Black Out for

SCENE 2

On stage—Occasional chair LC by backcloth
  Table C 2 feet from backcloth
  Stool L of table
  Pallet of straw L of stool

SCENE 3

To be set quietly during previous Scene

On stage—Hollow tree-trunk from Court Scene set the reverse way LC
  Inside Tree: A quantity of dead leaves

Off stage—Brown horse
  Profile Barge. *On it at front:* horse's nosebag and 10 yards of old trick
    line loosely coiled
  A piece of rope fastened on to platform to tie off with

Hand properties—Two school satchels for LUCY and HAROLD RABBIT

ACT IV

SCENE 1

On stage—Packing-case table RC. *On it:* one or two small sheets of cartridge-
          paper, duster, two or three pistols, 1 cutlass,
          3 pairs of handcuffs
  On floor by table: three sets of equipment ready for BADGER, MOLE and
    TOAD to put on, made up as follows: 2 shoulder-straps each, 1 belt
    each, 1 Thermos flask each, 2 pistols each, 1 pouch each, 1 cutlass
    each, 1 policeman's whistle each on cord to go round neck
    (separate) and 1 stick with bladder each
  Keg R of table
  Cupboard up C
  In cupboard: two or three ginger-beer bottles (one with loose cork), a
    few biscuits, old sauce bottles, folded sack, brush and pan
  1 rustic chair up LC (from Act II)
  Looking-glass on flat R above door
  Keg up LC
  Camp bed (from Act II, Scene 2) down LC
  On it: straw pallet, pillow with canvas cover painted moss-green
    colour, and piece of old sailcloth for bedcover

Hand properties—Old leaves and soil for TOAD's pocket
          1 special pistol with half blank charge for TOAD

During Black Out have ready one complete set of Equipment as before with:
  1 cudgel, 1 stick and bladder, 1 policeman's whistle on cord, 1 pair of handcuffs, 1 sheet of paper for RAT off L, 2 lanterns alight ready to hand to
  BADGER and RAT

SCENE 2

No properties on stage for this Scene

During this Scene strike Scene 1, Rat's House, and set (all to be done very quietly)

SCENE 3

On stage—Curtains for openings on flats down R and down L
  Curtains hanging behind opening up RC on cut-cloth
  Long table up C
  Behind table: large armchair, small bench R of chair, small bench L
    of chair
  Armchair R of table
  Armchair L of table
  Long bench in front of table

On table: 12 goblets, 4 prison dishes, 1 dozen soft oranges on dish, 1 dozen bananas on dish, 1 dozen rolls, 1 lobster on gilt dish, 12 gilt plates, 2 gilt jugs, 1 joint of beef on dish, 2 gilt bowls of mixed fruits, 1 wooden hammer (centre of table)

Hand properties—Old foolscap envelopes for TOAD
         1 pencil for one of the children
         Laurel wreath for CHIEF WEASEL

Off stage—Spare sticks and bladder

Have ready to set in Black Out Prologue:
   Ground row and grass matting up R corner
   1 rug

EPILOGUE

LC as in Prologue
Ground row grass matting and basket of flowers RC as in Prologue
1 rug

LIGHTING PLOT

PROLOGUE

Floats—RC circuit, amber and pink
No. 1 *Batten*—1 circuit amber and pink
L *Perch*—1 focus amber (No. 3) on to grass mat RC
R *Perch*—1 focus amber (No. 3) on to log LC
At cut: "Quick! Hide!"—Slow Black Out on resistance

ACT I

At cue: Bring in slowly on resistance
Floats—1 circuit white, a circuit amber and pink
Nos. 1, 2, 3, 4 *Battens*—1 circuit white, 1 circuit amber and pink
No. 5 *Batten*—1 circuit white, 2 circuits blue
4 lengths white and amber circuits behind cut-cloth
6 lengths white and amber circuits behind ground row
L *Perch*—2 focus amber (No. 19)
R *Perch*—2 focus pink (No. 21)
4 spot lamps over No. 1 batten:
    No. 1 on log LC
    No. 2 on door in cut-cloth up LC
    No. 3 on stage C in line with No. 2 wood wings
    No. 4 in cut-cloth up C
1 floor lamp, amber (No. 17), on backcloth up L
1 flood lamp, amber (No. 19), on backcloth up L
1 flood lamp, amber (No. 17), on backcloth up R
1 flood lamp, amber (No. 19), on backcloth up R
At cue: "My own view—since asked."—Bring in blues in floats and Nos. 1,
    2, 3, 4 battens and change all perches slowly to No. 18 blue
At cue: Take everything out quickly in resistance except blue floats, battens and
    perches
At cue: Lightning effect on backcloth up L
At cue: All lights up in 20 seconds as at the beginning of the Act

ACT II

SCENE 1

L *Perch*—Focus blue (No. 24) with two obscures ½ up with both lamps
R *Perch*—Focus blue (No. 24) with two obscures ½ up with both lamps. All
    4 lamps to keep off cloth and focus across stage
Snow effect from front of house at rise of Curtain and all through the scene
1 hand lantern alight ready off R for RAT
Perches and snow effect to check out on fall of Curtain

SCENE 2

Set Lights as follows before rise of Curtain:
    Floats—1 circuit white, 1 circuit amber and pink
    No. 1 *Batten*—1 circuit amber and pink. 1 circuit blue
    Nos. 2, 3, 4, 5—Blue circuits
    No. 1 *Spot Lamp*—White
    L *Perch*—Top lamp amber (No. 3), bottom lamp pink (No. 21)
    R *Perch*—Top lamp amber (No. 3), bottom lamp pink (*No.* 21)
    1 flood lamp, blue (No. 18), up L on backcloth
    1 flood lamp, blue (No. 18), up R on backcloth
    6 lengths, blue behind ground row

1 stage focus lamp, blue (No. 10), from L through window c
1 red lamp behind linen in fireplace up LC
1 log fire not alight on stage in front of linen fireplace
2 hanging lanterns R and L of window c, alight.
1 hand lantern with own battery, on stick, ready off L
At cue: Black Out on Switch

SCENE 3

(The same set)

Set Lights as follows before rise of Curtain:
Floats—1 circuit white, 1 circuit amber and pink
Nos. 1, 2, 3, 4 *Battens*—White circuits
No. 5 *Batten*—1 white circuit, 2 blue circuits
No. 1 Spot—White
L *Perch*—Both lamps amber (No. 17)
R *Perch*—Both lamps amber (No. 17)
6 lengths white and amber circuits behind ground row
2 hanging lanterns, not alight

ACT III

SCENE 1

Floats—1 circuit white, 1 circuit amber and pink
Nos. 1, 2, 3, 4 *Battens*—White circuits
No. 5 *Batten*—1 white circuit, 2 blue circuits
4 spot lamps, white
L *Perch*—Both lamps amber (No. 17)
R *Perch*—Both lamps amber (No. 17)
6 lengths white and amber circuits behind ground row
1 flood stage lamp white L and R in backcloth
At cue: Black Out on Switch

SCENE 2

Set Lights as follows before rise of Curtain:
Floats—1 circuit amber and pink (RC section only), 1 circuit blue
L *Perch*—Top lamp amber (No. 17)
R *Perch*—Both lamps blue (No. 18)
Stage L—(In first entrance) 1 flood lamp amber (No. 17) on and off at cues
Black Out on Switch

SCENE 3

Set Lights as follows before rise of Curtain:
Floats ⎫
Battens ⎬same as Act III, Scene 1
Perches ⎭
4 lengths blue behind No. 1 ground row
6 lengths white and amber circuits behind second ground row
2 flood lamps, white, on backcloth up L
2 flood lamps, white, on backcloth up R

ACT IV

SCENE 1

Same Lighting as Act II, Scene 2 plus

1 length amber on front of ground row
N.B.—But *no* red lamp for fire
         no stage focus L
         no lantern on stick off L
         no lantern for RAT
             Black Out on Switch

SCENE 2

Set Lights as follows before rise of Curtain:
Floats—1 circuit blue.
L *Perch*—Both lamps blue (No. 24), $\frac{1}{2}$ up
R *Perch*—Both lamps blue (No. 24), $\frac{1}{2}$ up

Black Out on Switch

SCENE 3

At signal bring in on switch:
Floats—1 circuit white, 1 circuit amber and pink
Nos. 1, 2, 3, 4 *Battens*—1 circuit white, 1 circuit amber and pink
4 spot lamps, white
Both perches—2 lamps each side pink (No. 5)
3 stage flood lamps, blue (No. 24), behind small window backcloth
Black Out slowly on resistance

EPILOGUE

L *Perch*—1 lamp, amber (No. 3), $\frac{1}{2}$ up slowly to open
No. 1 *Batten*—Amber and pink circuit, $\frac{1}{4}$, after perch on
1 focus stage lamp, white with funnel, off R behind opening in R flat to come and go off at cue
1 log fire with own resistance to be brought on to c during Black Out and to come in at cue
NOTE—All perches, spots, and stage lamps to be obscured throughout

A NOTE ABOUT THE SCENERY

The illustrations of Scenery represent the sets and cloths which were used in the London production and are obviously beyond the capabilities of many amateur organizations. The illustrations are intended as a help.

Scenery of so elaborate a nature is of course optional.

COSTUME PLOT

MOLE—Dark grey moleskin trousers and tunic with tail, dark grey moleskin cap, coloured muffler, handkerchief, old light grey short Norfolk jacket, shoes.

RAT—Trousers and body water-rat colour, lightish blue blazer with gilt buttons, handkerchief, white kitchen apron, socks to match costume, dark blue sailor's cap, animal rat headpiece, tail, gum boots, sou'wester and oilskins, shoes.

BADGER—Skin trousers and tunic right up to neck with tail, handkerchief, animal headpiece (black and white), tartan shooting coat with leathers.

TOAD—Handkerchief, shiny green top-hat, head skin, green "Johnny Walker" coat, toad legs and body, and body right up to neck, green socks, shoes.
   Woman's dress: 2 dresses, 2 coarse aprons, 2 bonnets with feathers and 2 shawls.

ALFRED—White horse costume.

JUDGE—Wig, gown and cape, 2 pairs black stockings, black cloth breeches, black sash and 1 pair of black pumps.

GAOLER—Black tights, black jersey decorated with red skull and crossbones on front, black velvet mask, skull-cap, black buckle shoes.

POLICEMAN—Lightish blue tunic and trousers, policeman's helmet (painted blue to match tunic), boots.

USHER—Town Crier's Costume: Darkish brown coat and cape with gold braidings, knee-breeches and 2 pairs of white stockings, stiff conical hat in dark brown with band of lighter brown, black buckle shoes, 2 pairs gloves, 3 cravats.

CHIEF WEASEL—Weasel's costume with laurel wreath and gold Sam-Browne belt added, 2 pairs of socks to match costume, shoes.

CHIEF FERRET—Costume with silver fillet and silver Sam-Browne belt added, 2 pairs of socks to match costume.

DUCK—Costume and headdress.

FOX—Costume and headdress.

TURKEY—Costume and headdress.

MARIGOLD—Attractive child's frock.

NURSE—Grey frock, grey headdress and stockings, grey shoes.

WASHERWOMAN—Black woollen shawl, black felt boots, woollen stockings, red flannel petticoat with large pocket and padded white camisole.

BARGE-WOMAN—Bright striped dress, orange coloured handkerchief for head, unbleached apron, white stockings, boots.

PHOEBE—White skirt with pink roses, pink satin polonaise with fichu, two wristlets of roses, pink shoes and stockings and shepherdess hat.

WHITE RABBIT—Costume.

LUCY RABBIT—Rabbit costume with small pinafore and tam-o'-shanter.

HAROLD RABBIT—Rabbit costume with small blue Eton coat.

MAMA RABBIT—Rabbit costume with straw hat.

FIELD MICE—Fawn costumes with long tails.

RABBITS—Brown costumes.

STOATS—Fawn costumes with white fronts.

WEASELS—Beige costumes.

FERRETS—White costumes with black-tipped tails.

SQUIRRELS—Grey costumes with bushy tails.

BARGE HORSE—Brown horse costume.

DOWN BY THE WILLOWS
(*Drop Cloth of Transparent Gauze*)

THE RIVER BANK

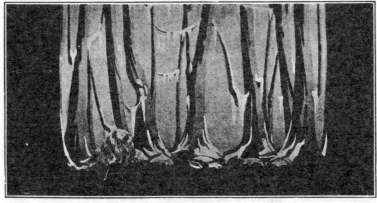

THE WILD WOOD
(*Drop Cloth*)

BADGER'S HOUSE

THE COURT-HOUSE

THE DUNGEON
(Front Cloth)

THE CANAL BANK

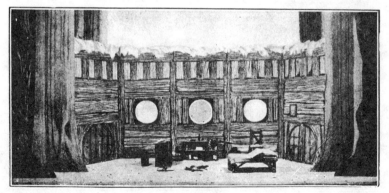

RAT'S HOUSE

THE UNDERGROUND PASSAGE
(Front Cloth)

THE BANQUETING-ROOM AT TOAD HALL

MADE AND PRINTED IN GREAT BRITAIN BY
LATIMER TREND & COMPANY LTD PLYMOUTH

MADE IN ENGLAND